We are indeed much more than what we eat,

But what we eat can nevertheless help us

To be much more than what we are.

. . .

**Adelle Davis**

# *Truly* **Tasty**

First published in 2010 by Atrium
Atrium is an imprint of Cork University Press
Youngline Industrial Estate, Pouladuff Road, Togher, Cork, Ireland

British Library Cataloguing in Publication Data

A CIP catalogue record for this book is available from the British Library.

ISBN 978-185594-214-1

Editor: **Lizzie Gore-Grimes**

© recipes: **The Chefs**
© chef interviewing: **Brian Moore**
© Illustrations: **Orlagh Murphy**
© photography: **Hugh McElveen**
Additional photography: © Orla Keeshan p. 262; © Eva Power p. 274;
© Donagh Glavin p. 288; © Brian Moore p. 180; © RTÉ p. 260; © Ronnie Norton p. 114.
© Irish Nutrition and Dietetic Institute p. xx–xxiii, p. 216–217, p. 282–285 and Coding System.

Book design and typesetting: Anú Design, Tara
Printed in Malta by Gutenberg Press
For all Atrium books visit www.corkuniversitypress.com

# Truly Tasty

OVER 100 SPECIAL RECIPES CREATED BY IRELAND'S TOP
CHEFS FOR ADULTS LIVING WITH KIDNEY DISEASE

Editor: Lizzie Gore-Grimes

Photography: Hugh McElveen

ATRIUM

This book is most sincerely dedicated to:

The donor who gave me the most precious gift of all – continued life. That extraordinary person, and their family, are always in my thoughts.

To everyone who is living with kidney disease; I understand only too well the challenging journey you are on.

To my wonderful mum and dad, for their love and support over the years. You are an inspiration in everything that I do. And to my fantastic family and friends who were, and always are, there for me.

To the outstanding renal healthcare team, led by consultant nephrologist Dr Liam Plant, at Cork University Hospital for their quality care, support, kindness and advice through my time on dialysis and on to this very day. Also to Beaumont Hospital for their outstanding transplant care.

To Dr Mary Dunphy for her overwhelming care and friendship and for constantly being by my side. And finally to my late cousin, Peter Twomey, who showed me the true meaning of courage and hope and reconfirmed by belief that the only truly important thing in life is...

Family, friends and community

## CHEFS

contents

Contents

### KEY TO ICONS

 CHEF'S NOTE

 DIETITIAN'S NOTE

 LOW FAT

### ABBREVIATIONS USED IN THIS BOOK

| | |
|---|---|
| 1 tsp | 1 teaspoon |
| 1 tbsp | 1 tablespoon |
| ml | millilitre |
| lt | litre |
| pt | pint |
| g | gram |
| oz | ounce |
| lb | pound |

# Acknowledgements

This book could not have been written without the combined efforts of so many kind people. My sincere thanks go to...

Brian Moore, a true gentleman, for his encouraging words and unstinting support and belief. His interviews with the chefs are a terrific addition to the book.

A very special heartfelt thank you to the renal dietitians from the Irish Nutrition & Dietetic Institute. I thank them for their overwhelming support, expertise and the countless hours they put in analysing recipes for this book. Without their incredible dedication and invaluable input this book would never have been written or published. *Go raibh míle maith agaibh.*

To all the wonderful chefs who contributed so generously to this publication. I can't thank them enough for their co-operation and endless patience with my constant emails, manipulation of ingredients and for giving of their time so graciously. In particular, sincere thanks to Richie Wilson, executive chef at the Morrison Hotel, Dublin, Peter Merrigan, head chef at Avoca, Rathcoole, and to Philip Geraghty and Niamh Donohoe at Bosch, who helped me at every turn with overwhelming support and kindness. I am extremely grateful to you all.

I would like to express my deep gratitude to my supporting editorial team, as the book would not have been possible without the combined efforts of:

Lizzie Gore-Grimes, food writer and editor, a true professional. I thank her for her enthusiasm, understanding, sheer commitment, endless patience and for her constant support and advice, which helped me move forward at some challenging times. To Orlagh Murphy, for her imagination, creativity and skill in creating a magnificent book cover and adding wonderful illustrative touches throughout the book. To Hugh McElveen, food photographer, for his amazing photographs. He really captured the phrase "you eat with your eyes". I thank him for his professionalism, perfectionism and for making hectic days run smoothly with humour and patience. And finally I would like to thank Orla Broderick for her meticulous recipe proofing. *I wonder, guys, is it too early to chat to you all about my next book idea!*

To my publisher Mike Collins and all the team at Cork University Press, who never pushed us to work faster than we could cope with. Their input, guidance and support in putting this book together was much appreciated. A sincere thanks to Karen Carty for her unique, creative imagination in designing *Truly Tasty* and for putting up with our many requests.

Finally, and very importantly, a sincere thank you to our sponsors, in particular our principal sponsor, Abbott Ireland, Bosch, National Lottery, Shire Pharmaceuticals Ireland Ltd, Amgen Ireland Ltd and Shamrock Foods Ltd for their support in helping produce this innovative cookbook. To Fiona Foley & Co., solicitors, for their invaluable legal advice and guidance and sincere heartfelt thanks to Breda Dooley, PR consultant, for her passion, belief and unstinting support. We could not have done this without you all.

All proceeds from the sale of *Truly Tasty* go to the Irish Kidney Association.

***We did it!***

*Valerie Twomey*

An introduction from...

# VALERIE TWOMEY

Founder of *Truly Tasty*

Medically speaking, I have been through a lot in my life. I was diagnosed with type 1 diabetes mellitus at the age of 13 and, over the years, I have had a number of eye operations, quadruple heart bypass surgery and a kidney transplant, but, in the words of Elton John, *"I'm still standing, better than I ever did"*.

I reached end-stage kidney disease in 2004 and, strange as this may sound, I was quite pleased to be starting dialysis because I had been feeling miserable as the toxins were building up in my blood. I knew that dialysis would remove these poisonous waste products and help me feel much better. Of course, when I initially heard the words "dialysis" and "kidney transplant", I was shocked and scared. But I accepted it quite quickly, thanks to the terrific support of the renal healthcare team led by consultant nephrologist Dr Liam Plant, my general practitioner Dr Mary Dunphy, and the Irish Kidney Association.

I started on home dialysis (automated peritoneal dialysis or APD), during which a machine performed my dialysis overnight, but after sixteen months this form of treatment became less efficient. As a result, my dialysis was inadequate and my blood pressure was beginning to rise; I felt nauseous on a daily basis. At this stage, I had to change to haemodialysis and so I attended the dialysis unit at Cork University Hospital three days a week.

At the beginning, I struggled with this treatment and found it difficult but thankfully Eileen Phelan (CNM2) with her uplifting words, humour, kindness and endless support helped me to settle in. In the words of Mother Theresa,

*"Kind words can be short and easy to speak, but their echoes are truly endless."*

This period of treatment was a challenging time for me. There were many ups and downs but I felt very lucky at least to have the option of dialysis while I waited on a transplant. I was determined not to let dialysis take over my life. So, changes had to be made. It took me a while to become fully aware of my health limitations and to learn to readjust. A thought that kept me going through this time was, *"Life is not the way it's supposed to be; it's the way it is. How we deal with it is what makes the difference."* I simply took one day at a time and remained positive.

When I had difficult days, I just wished they would pass quickly and that the next day would be a better one – but I always had hope. I remember reading an article written by Christopher Reeve on how to remain positive, and the following words really jumped out at me: *"Once you choose hope, anything is possible."*

When I was going through haemodialysis, I had an epiphany. I realised that I wanted to do something to make a difference, in some small way, for other people with kidney disease and their families going through this difficult journey.

I also wanted to thank my wonderful healthcare team at Cork University Hospital – Dr Liam Plant, Dr Sinead Kinsella, the home dialysis nurses, the haemodialysis nurses, care assistants and especially I wanted to thank Fiona Byrne and Irene Lynch, the renal dietitians who looked after me – for all their hard work in keeping me on the right track with my own renal diet programme. I know there were times at the beginning when I wasn't the most compliant patient! But I did see for myself that the dietary restrictions play a vital role in the successful long-term management of chronic kidney disease. I knew then that this was the message I wanted to help reinforce.

It is important that all people with kidney disease control the build-up of waste products in their blood. So, they need to follow a tailor-made dietary programme to ensure that their diet is adequate in protein, low in salt and, where necessary, low in phosphate and potassium. Sticking to this diet plan sounded okay to me at first until I started looking into what was in the foods I was used to eating. The things I found hardest to give up were my daily homemade fruit and vegetable juices, bran flakes, bananas, pine nuts, creamy mashed potatoes (only boiled once!), diet cola and those tasty bacon butties. But I stuck with it.

Then, in June 2006, I received the most precious gift of all – that of continued life – from a loving stranger, and I am so privileged to have this opportunity to express my sincere gratitude and deepest appreciation to them and their family. No words can describe the heartfelt thanks I feel towards my kind donor and their loved ones. Now I knew I had to give something back. I had the idea for this book bubbling away in my head and now it was time for action. When you are diagnosed with kidney disease, life as you know it simply changes. Suddenly you and your family are faced with a new way of living, which certainly can be quite difficult, in particular when it comes to food and fluid restrictions. Trying to create tasty meals that all the family can enjoy can be frustrating and difficult.

I felt there must be a way for people on the renal diet to enjoy recipes for special occasions, entertaining and Sunday lunches, while staying within the dietary guidelines; *truly tasty* recipes that could be enjoyed by the rest of the family and friends too.

Once I mentioned the plan to the renal team at Cork University Hospital – consultant nephrologists Dr Liam Plant and Dr Joseph Eustace, clinical specialist renal dietitian Fiona Byrne, renal nurse specialist Abina Harrington – and Mr Mark Murphy, chief executive of the Irish Kidney Association, I was thrilled with the encouragement and support they gave me to take the project forward.

Shortly after this, I was introduced to Brian Moore, a journalist with a great passion for food, who inspired me further with his enthusiasm for the project. His help in contacting chefs and interviewing them for this book was invaluable.

When we got in touch with the chefs, I was blown away by their immediate kindness and willingness to give up their time to compile recipes suitable for people with kidney disease.

I believe that the delicious recipes they have given us for this book will inspire and motivate the renal community to enjoy great-tasting food while staying within their dietary guidelines. I hope that the book will also be an inspiring guide and reference for family members, carers and friends who wish to prepare delicious meals in the confidence that they are cooking the correct food.

Another key goal for me is that the book will increase and strengthen organ donor awareness, as it was only through the kindness of such a donor that I got my second chance at life – and had the opportunity to bring you this unique book.

Needless to say, I could not have done it without the support of my wonderful parents, my special family – particularly my sister Karen – my great friends, and everyone in my local community, to whom I am eternally grateful for all their kindness and for always being there for me. Special thanks also to the Irish Kidney Association and to Deirdre Thompson, my pharmacist, for looking out for me. As for the overwhelming high-quality care, support and kindness that I constantly received from Dr Liam Plant, Dr Sinead Kinsella and every member of the renal multidisciplinary team, *go raibh míle maith agaibh.*

*"I may not have been blessed with good health but certainly I am blessed with fantastic parents, family, friends and a top-quality, caring healthcare team."*

A word from...

# BRIAN MOORE

While working for the *Carlow Nationalist*, I was asked to cover a story about the Irish Blood Transfusion Service's push to get more people to give blood. When I arrived at the clinic and began to chat to the doctors and nurses for the article, they asked me if I would like to give blood, to "walk the walk after talking the talk", so to speak. So up I jumped on to the trolley and rolled up my sleeve. The nurse came over to take my blood pressure and that's when it all went a bit mad.

After three attempts to take a blood pressure reading, the nurse called for one of the doctors to take a look at me. It turned out that my blood pressure was very, very high and the doctors recommended that I be admitted to hospital for tests.

So, off to hospital I went and, after many tests, I was told that one of my kidneys wasn't functioning at all and the other one was working at only about ten per cent. Now, this all came as a complete shock to me because I was, or at least thought I was, healthy. I was six feet tall and weighed ten stone. In fact, I had never felt so good!

Today, I am on the kidney transplant list but I have yet to start dialysis, so diet is a very important part of staying healthy for me. I would encourage everybody to have a full health check at least once a year and to always carry an organ donor card.

When Valerie Twomey approached me to interview the chefs for *Truly Tasty*, I was delighted to get involved. Working on this book has given me an insight into what amazing people like Valerie have been through. I can't underestimate the positive effect that Val has had on my life in general over the past year and a half.

I love food. I always have. Food is to me what sport is to most people; I like to plan what I will be cooking for dinner while I am eating lunch. When I was told that I would need a kidney transplant, all I asked about was what foods I would have to give up.

While working on this book, I have fulfilled a dream to interview my food heroes, and in doing so I hope I may have inspired others, in the same boat as myself, to see food as part of the road to recovery. For me, a book like this gives hope to anyone who is about to start, or is already on, dialysis. The chefs in this book have proven that you can enjoy great food while on the renal diet. Their skill and expertise have created dishes that are tasty, full of flavour, and fun to make and eat. I hope you enjoy them.

*Brian Moore interviewed all the chefs in this book.*

xiv

A word from...

# DR LIAM PLANT

National Clinical Director

## Eating Well with Kidney Problems

One cannot enter a bookstore today without encountering a host of tomes on diet, nutrition and the culinary arts. From the glitziest offerings of the celebrity chef to the modest guide on *Budget Cooking for Singletons*, there is certainly no lack of choice. It seems that we cannot avoid advice on how to eat well and how to enjoy eating.

For some, however, eating well and enjoying eating may not be quite such an easy task. For those with long-term kidney problems, diet is an important aspect of their care. It is not a simple process to switch from a diet with no real limitations to one with many. Knowing "what's in that dish" is not something that comes easily. Preparation of a meal suitable for adults with kidney disease is one step; preparation of a kidney-friendly meal that is also delicious may be a considerably harder step to master.

This book, assembled with trademark enthusiasm by Val Twomey, aims to make these steps simple. For those of you with kidney problems, this book will help you develop the skills you need to make the most of the many wonderful foods that are suitable to your diet – whilst avoiding the foods that are not. I congratulate her.

Move over, Jamie!

A word from…

# MARK MURPHY

Chief Executive, Irish Kidney Association

**The Irish Kidney Association (IKA)** was formed in 1978 by patients for patients and their families. The IKA provides help to people newly diagnosed with end-stage kidney disease, as well as those receiving treatment. The IKA's patient support is unique in that it comes from a group of people who really understand the challenges encountered when living with end-stage kidney disease.

Members can receive assistance in the form of information through a range of publications on kidney disease such as complimentary patient manuals and *Support*, the quarterly IKA magazine. In addition, educational seminars on various aspects of kidney disease are organised. The association recognises the importance of psychological and financial support at a traumatic period in a patient's life, and offers counselling services. Financial patient aid is also available in emergencies to cover costs such as electricity, telephone, clothing and travel.

The IKA is a national association with branches throughout Ireland offering peer support. It is the only voluntary organisation working solely in the interest of patients with end-stage kidney disease.

Today, there are almost two million people worldwide living with failed kidneys. One-third are transplanted and two-thirds are undergoing dialysis treatment – there are two forms of dialysis: "haemodialysis" (the most common form) and "peritoneal dialysis".

The development of the haemodialysis machine in the 1950s and 1960s, followed by the development of kidney transplantation, for the first time offered an effective treatment for individuals affected by end-stage kidney disease. The first dialysis machine, also known as the artificial kidney, was invented by a Dutch doctor, Willem J. Kolff. His first successful dialysis treatment took place in 1945, in a rural hospital in the town of Kampen in the Netherlands. These treatments have continued to improve over the years, with the advancement of medical technologies and the discovery of immunosuppressive drugs to prevent organ rejection. Continued research is vital and an important additional purpose of the IKA is to support, encourage and promote research into the incidence, prevention and treatment of kidney disease, fostering a better understanding and knowledge of this major health problem through public and professional awareness programmes.

As a voluntary body, the IKA depends mainly upon fundraising to meet its major commitment to financing medical research, public education, meeting the needs of people living with kidney disease and to distributing organ donor cards nationally. The IKA organises national donor awareness campaigns four times a year and works tirelessly to promote public awareness all year round through national advertising campaigns and the like. The IKA recognises the importance and value of promoting a healthy lifestyle through regular exercise and sport. Consequently, a sports programme was established, open to all people on dialysis and organ transplant recipients.

More and more people are in need of dialysis treatment every year, so they must face not only the challenge of the treatment but also a dramatic change in lifestyle. Adhering to the renal diet brings a further challenge – but help is at hand. With this unique book, Valerie Twomey has worked with Ireland's best chefs and the top renal dietitians in the country to produce an inspirational cookery book complete with recipes that adults on a renal diet can enjoy for special occasions.

www.ika.ie

Developed for chronic kidney disease patients, these specially designed Abbott dialysis support packs contain a travel bag, drinks beaker, umbrella and eye mask. The Abbott dialysis support packs are distributed to specialist dialysis units around the country.

# Abbott Ireland

# Proudly supporting Truly Tasty

Abbott Ireland, one of Ireland's leading healthcare companies, is proud to support the publication of a special cookbook, **Truly Tasty**. This cookbook is unique in that all the recipes included are specifically designed for adults following a renal diet and have been expertly compiled by Valerie Twomey, created by Ireland's top chefs and meticulously analysed by the Irish Nutrition & Dietetic Institute. Offering a host of easily accessible recipes for patients and families, **Truly Tasty** provides a fresh take on enjoying inspiring ideas for tasty meals for those following a renal diet.

There's no doubt that the renal diet is a challenge and requires planning, imagination and practical ideas. We are delighted that so many top Irish chefs have lent their expertise and gourmet flair to create a selection of delicious and original recipes for all to enjoy. Derry Clarke, Neven Maguire, Rachel Allen and Clodagh McKenna are just a few of the well-known culinary masters who have devised special recipes for this book.

Abbott has a long and proud history in Ireland of producing medicines, diagnostic equipment and nutritional products. Our first site opened in Dublin in 1946 and since then, we have grown to become one of Ireland's largest employers, with sites located in Tipperary, Cavan, Donegal, Longford, Mayo, Sligo and Dublin. We are delighted to support **Truly Tasty** and we would like to take this opportunity especially to thank Valerie Twomey who has put such a huge amount of time, energy and enthusiasm into developing this book.

*"Truly Tasty" is a credit to everyone who has been involved. We hope you enjoy trying out these tasty and imaginative recipes for yourself. Happy cooking!*

**Irish Nutrition and Dietetic Institute**

A word from...

# THE RENAL DIETITIANS

## A Guide to Using this Book

As dietitians, we are extremely aware that the renal diet places challenging restrictions on adults with kidney disease, and we often struggle to come up with new and interesting recipe suggestions. When Valerie Twomey gave us the opportunity to tap into Ireland's top culinary talent to create new and delicious dishes suitable for adults on a renal diet, it was an opportunity not to be missed.

Good cookery books are invaluable for special occasions. Now we have a cookery book that is perfect for entertaining or for planning that special family meal for adults with chronic kidney disease (CKD) or those on dialysis. Many chefs have provided a starter, main course and dessert. **However**, for most chefs, you will not have enough in your daily allowances to have all three courses. For some chefs you may only have enough in your allowances to pick one course. You will have to pick and choose recipes depending on your daily allowances.

There are a lot of tasty recipes in this book but please use it carefully as part of your overall diet plan. It is important to take a few minutes to read through the introduction so that you can get the most out of this book.

## Diet and your kidneys

The aim of the renal diet is to make sure that your diet is balanced, as well as to avoid the build-up of waste products in your blood. A balanced diet means that you are getting enough nourishment to keep you healthy.

## One size does not fit all!

Each adult with CKD is unique. Dietary needs vary with body size, age, the type of dialysis you require, other medical conditions that you may have and the amount of kidney function that you have remaining.

As a result, you have been given a diet sheet that suits your particular needs. Check your diet sheet, for your allowances, to help you pick and choose which recipes you can have.

## Coding System

A coding system with the number of fruit and vegetable portions, the number of potatoes, as well as protein and dairy exchanges is found at the bottom of each recipe. Recipes that are low in fat have been coded using (LF) and these meals can be included more often in your diet (again within your allowances).

It is important to remember that the codes are based on one serving or portion from each dish or dessert.

It should be noted that the coding system in this book is based on the Irish Nutrition and Dietetic Institute renal diet sheet and the Irish (ROI) method of educating adults with CKD and those on dialysis. Before using this book, you are advised to discuss the recipes with your dietitian.

## Protein

Protein foods such as meat, fish, chicken and eggs are very important for good nutrition. The amount of protein you need depends on your stage of kidney disease, your size and whether or not you are on dialysis. Your dietitian can help you plan how much protein you need to eat.

We have used protein exchanges to help you get the right amount of protein each day. As a general rule 1 protein exchange is approximately equal to 1oz of cooked meat. Therefore, if you have been advised to eat 4oz meat or equivalent per day, this is equal to 4 protein exchanges. If you have been advised to eat 6oz meat, this is equal to 6 protein exchanges and so on. Each recipe has the number of protein exchanges per portion at the end of the recipe. Remember to adjust the portion size to match your daily protein allowance.

## Potassium

Potassium is a mineral found in food. With kidney failure, the amount of potassium in the body can rise too high. This is dangerous as it can cause a heart attack. **If you have been advised to follow a low potassium diet, it is essential that you get further advice from your dietitian.**

If you are on a potassium restriction, you will need to restrict your fruit, vegetable and potato intake. In addition, potatoes must be boiled (as per p. 282) to reduce the potassium content. You will also need to avoid foods that are high in potassium. (Check your diet sheet or talk to your dietitian)

Each recipe has been clearly coded at the end to indicate how many portions of fruit, vegetables and/or the number of potatoes it contains. Please check with your dietitian what your daily allowance is for each of these foods.

*Potatoes*

Boiling potatoes to reduce the potassium content (see p. 282) removes a lot of vitamins as well. **For this reason we do not recommend you serve potatoes cooked in this way for the entire family.**

*Herbs and Spices*

The chefs have included fresh herbs and spices in many of the recipes and they are a wonderful way of boosting the flavour of food, especially on a no added salt diet. A word of warning: if you are on a potassium restriction, herbs and spices contain potassium and therefore should only be used sparingly. We have analysed the content of each recipe and, in some cases, where a lot of fresh herbs are included, we have counted them as part of a vegetable portion.

## Fat

Reducing fat in your diet has the benefit of both helping to reduce your blood fat levels as well as reducing calorie and energy intakes. Recipes which are lower in fat and more suitable for healthy eating are marked (LF).

Like many desserts served in restaurants, quite a few desserts include ingredients such as cream, and so are high in fat. Therefore, some of the recipes will not be suitable for you if you have been advised to reduce your fat intake.

## Salt

Reducing your salt intake is particularly important for blood pressure management.

Indeed one of the main healthy eating messages right now is that the entire population should reduce their salt intake. Controlling blood pressure is even more important if you have CKD. We have avoided salty foods in the recipes. Remember not to add salt at the table.

## Phosphate

Keeping blood phosphate under control is extremely important for your health if you have kidney disease. Two ways to limit your phosphate intake include:

1. Avoid high phosphate foods
2. Limit your daily intake of dairy foods

These recipes have avoided high phosphate foods and have been coded to tell you the number of dairy exchanges they contain per portion. 1 dairy exchange is equal to 200ml of milk or 1oz cheese or 125g yoghurt.

If you have been prescribed phosphate binders it is important to take them with your meals.

## Dietary Allowances

When you pick a recipe, you must remember what other food you plan to eat during the day and make sure that you are not exceeding your allowances. To help you pick and choose suitable recipes, we have included a quick analysis summary of each recipe on p. xxv. We have also included on the bookmark a space for you to fill in your own allowances.

## *If in any doubt, talk to your dietitian.*

"Truly Tasty is indeed a perfect special occasions cookbook. We hope you enjoy it".

Irish Nutrition & Dietetic Institute

# FOOD SAFETY

Good food hygiene is important for everyone. It is even more important for those who have a chronic illness such as kidney disease. It is essential if you have had a transplant and are on immunosuppressive medications or if you are pregnant.

We have included some food safety tips below that are relevant to the recipes included in this book.

1. Cook all food including meat, chicken, fish and eggs thoroughly.

   **How to check that meats are properly cooked**
   - When you pierce the thickest part of the meat with a fork or skewer the **juices should run clear**. For a whole chicken or other bird, the thickest part is the leg between the drumstick and the breast.
   - Cut the meat open with a clean knife to check it is **piping hot all the way through** – it should be steaming.
   - Meat changes colour when it is cooked. Make sure there is **no pink meat left**.
   - If you're cooking a very large dish, check it in a few places, because some parts of the dish may be less hot than others.

   If you are cooking a dish containing eggs, make sure you cook it until the food is piping hot all the way through.

2. Soft cheeses such as brie and goat's cheese should be made with pasteurised milk and cooked thoroughly. It should reach 70°C for 2 minutes or equivalent i.e. hot enough for long enough to ensure that the cheese is heated through thoroughly. All cheeses should be made with pasteurised milk.

3. Wash all salads including lettuce leaves, herbs, fruit and vegetables thoroughly just before you use them.

4. You should always use fresh produce and throw out food that has passed the "use by" or "best before" date. Make sure that your fridge is at 5°C or below.

Please note these food safety tips are not exhaustive. For more information, check the following websites: www.fsai.ie, www.safefood.eu, and www.eatwell.gov.uk. These websites are not specifically tailored for renal patients so if you have any queries about the information you find please contact your dietitian.

# Summary of
# Dietary Allowances

per portion of the recipe

# STARTERS

| Recipe | Chef/ Page Number | Fruit Portions | Vegetable Portions | Number of Potatoes | Protein Exchanges | Dairy Product Exchanges |
|---|---|---|---|---|---|---|
| Baked Cod Fillet, Sweet Mustard French Beans and Tomato Salsa **Low Fat** | Derry Clarke, p. 58 | | 1 | | 2 | |
| Brandade of White Fish | Paul Flynn, p. 151 | | ½ | ½ | 1½ | |
| Caramelised Onion, Roast Pepper and Brie Tartlet in Thyme Pastry | Tony Keogh, p. 244 | | 2 | | | ½ |
| Chicken Sausage with Red Pepper Jam | Patrick McLarnon, p. 142 | | ½ | | 1½ | |
| Chicken Soup **Low Fat** | Catherine Fulvio, p. 13 | | 2 | | 5 | |
| Cod and Salmon Tofu Cakes | Claire Nash, p. 35 | | ½ | | 3 | |
| Cottage Cheese, Pomegranate and Mint Bruschetta | Clodagh McKenna, p. 43 | ½ | | | | 1 |
| Courgette and Mint Soup | Leylie Hayes, p. 101 | | 2 | ½ | | |
| Courgette Carpaccio with Rocket and Parmesan | Rory O'Connell, p. 201 | | 2 | | | ½ |
| Courgette Fritters with Horseradish and Yoghurt Dip | Liz Moore, p. 109 | | 2 | | ½ | 1 |
| Fried Squid with Lime and Chilli Dressing | Georgina Campbell, p. 83 | ½ | | | 2 | |
| Grilled Courgette, Green Bean and Lentil Salad with Coriander, Mint and Yoghurt Dressing | Denis Cotter, p. 222 | | 2 | | ½ | |
| Melon and Raspberries with Cinnamon Jelly and Fresh Basil | Ross Lewis, p. 209 | 1½ | | | | |
| Onion Tart with Fresh Herb Cream Cheese | Domini Kemp, p. 67 | | 1½ | | | |
| Pan-Seared Tuna Fillet with Spicy Tropical Fruit Salsa | Dave Workowich, p. 264 | 2 | | | 3 | |

# STARTERS

| Recipe | Chef/ Page Number | Fruit Portions | Vegetable Portions | Number of Potatoes | Protein Exchanges | Dairy Product Exchanges |
|---|---|---|---|---|---|---|
| Poached Hen's Egg with Soft Polenta and Fresh Parmesan | Oliver Dunne, p. 135 | | | | 1 | |
| Poached Salmon Pancakes with Chive Cream Cheese | Kevin Dundon, p. 90 | | ½ | | 2 | ½ |
| Ravioli of Goat's Cheese with Fresh Basil and Sweet Plum Tomato Sauce | Noel McMeel, p. 126 | | 2 | | 1 | 1 |
| Risotto with Paprika and Red Pepper | David McCann, p. 51 | | 2 | | | 1 |
| Roast Pepper Hummus | Denis Cotter, p. 221 | | ½ | | ½ | |
| Roasted Pepper Tarts | Paula Mee, p. 167 | | 1½ | | | |
| Salad of Roast Beetroot with Garlic Cream Cheese | Dave Workowich, p. 266 | | 2 | | | |
| Savoy Cabbage and Barley Broth | Tony Keogh, p. 247 | | 2 | | | |
| Scotch Broth | Richie Wilson, p. 191 | | 1 | | 2½ | |
| Spiced Carrot and Pumpkin Soup | Peter Merrigan, p. 175 | | 2 | | | 1 |
| Tabouli | Brian Fallon, p. 5 | | 1 | | | |
| Vegetable and Tofu Spring Rolls with Sweet Chilli Sauce | Lorraine Fitzmaurice, p. 236 | | 1½ | | ½ | |
| Warm Lamb Salad with Yoghurt and Fresh Mint Dressing | Eugene McSweeney p. 75 | | 1 | | 1½ | |
| Warm Salad with Pear and White Cheddar Cheese | Neven Maguire, p. 117 | 1 | ½ | | | ½ |
| Watermelon Salad with Marinated Cheddar, Lime and Mint | Rachel Allen, p. 183 | 1 | | | | 1 |
| Za'atar Spiced Tuna with Creamed Cucumber Salad and Carrot and Ginger Dressing | Paula McIntyre, p. 158 | | 1 | | 2 | |

## MAIN COURSES

| Recipe | Chef/ Page Number | Fruit Portions | Vegetable Portions | Number of Potatoes | Protein Exchanges | Dairy Product Exchanges |
|---|---|---|---|---|---|---|
| Barbecued Leg of Lamb with Rosemary Marinade, Lacour Potatoes and Summer Salad | Richie Wilson, p. 192 | | 2 | 2 | 4½ | |
| Beef with Leeks, Crème Fraîche and Rice | Eugene McSweeney p. 76 | | 1 | | 3 | |
| Braised Chicken with Root Vegetables | Liz Moore, p. 110 | | 1½ | 1½ | 5 | |
| Chargrilled Fillet of Beef and Ratatouille **Low Fat** | Derry Clarke, p. 61 | | 2 | | 5 | |
| Chicken with Leeks and Tarragon | Rory O'Connell, p. 202 | | 1½ | | 4½ | |
| Cheese, Onion and Tomato Quiche | Catherine Leyden, p. 26 | | 1½ | | ½ | 1 |
| Dover Sole with Lemon and Parsley Butter, Olive Mash and Roast Baby Leeks | Georgina Campbell, p. 84 | | ½ | 2 | 4 | |
| Fillet of Pork Frascati with Basmati Rice | Claire Nash, p. 36 | | 1 | | 3 | ¼ |
| Fricassée of Summer Vegetables and Baked Tofu in a Sour Cream, Roast Garlic and Butterbean Sauce | Tony Keogh, p. 251 | | 2 | | 2 | |
| Grilled Paillard of Chicken with Penne Pasta, Courgettes, Peppers and Mint | Paula McIntyre, p. 160 | | 2 | | 5 | |
| Honey-Glazed Tofu with Rice Noodles and Greens in Ginger Coconut Sauce **Low Fat** | Denis Cotter, p. 225 | | 1½ | | 1½ | |
| Lamb Kebabs with Basmati Rice | Paula Mee, p. 168 | | 1 | | 3 | |
| Lasagne | Domini Kemp, p. 68 | | 2 | | 4½ | 1 |

## MAIN COURSES

| Recipe | Chef/ Page Number | Fruit Portions | Vegetable Portions | Number of Potatoes | Protein Exchanges | Dairy Product Exchanges |
|---|---|---|---|---|---|---|
| Medallions of Beef with Garlic Butter and Roasted Vegetables | Brian Fallon, p. 6 | | 2 | | 5 | |
| Moroccan Lamb Tagine with Lemon Couscous | Catherine Fulvio, p. 14 | | 1 | | 5 | |
| Pumpkin, Red Onion and Cheese Tortilla with Roast Garlic Aioli | Denis Cotter, p. 226 | | 1½ | | 2 | |
| Roast Aubergine and Gran Moravia Mousse with Beetroot Cream, Spiced Couscous, Green Beans, Pan-Fried Courgettes and Chickpeas | Tony Keogh, p. 248 | | 2 | | 1 | 1 |
| Roast Crown of Turkey with Sage and Onion Stuffing, Roast Carrots with Garlic and Parsley, Pan-Fried Brussel Sprouts with Nutmeg and Crispy Potatoes with Rosemary and Red Onion | Neven Maguire, p. 118 | | 2 | 1½ | 6 | |
| Roasted Fillet of Pork, Citrus Couscous, Roast Pepper and Courgettes | Oliver Dunne, p. 136 | ½ | 2 | | 4½ | |
| Roast Free-Range Chicken with Crispy Fried Potatoes and Carrot and Parsnip Mash | Noel McMeel, p. 128 | | 2 | 1½ | 5 | |
| Roast Pork Steak with leeks and Savoy Cabbage, Couscous and Curry Emulsion | David McCann, p. 52 | ½ | 2 | | 4 | |
| Roast Rib of Beef with Roast Vegetables | Stephen McAllister p. 270 | | 2 | 1½ | 5½ | |
| Roast Rump of Lamb with Tumeric Potatoes, Cucumber and Mint Sauce | Patrick McLarnon p. 144 | | 1 | 2 | 4 | ½ |

## MAIN COURSES

| Recipe | Chef/ Page Number | Fruit Portions | Vegetable Portions | Number of Potatoes | Protein Exchanges | Dairy Product Exchanges |
|---|---|---|---|---|---|---|
| Seared Fillet of Beef with Crispy Onions and Horseradish Dressing | Kevin Dundon, p. 93 | | 1 | | 3½ | |
| Shepherd's Pie | Stephen McAllister p. 272 | | 2 | 1½ | 3 | |
| Spicy Lamb Meatballs with Greek Salad and Mint Yoghurt | Rachel Allen, p. 184 | | 1½ | | 2½ | ½ |
| Summer Lemon and Pork Burger with Roasted Red Peppers and Rocket | Leylie Hayes, p. 102 | | 1½ | | 3½ | |
| Tagliatelle Pasta with Poached Fresh Salmon and Dill Cream | Peter Merrigan, p. 176 | | 1½ | | 2 | |
| Tarragon Place En Papillote Served with Julienne Vegetables and Chive Mash | Clodagh McKenna, p. 44 | | 2 | 2 | 3 | |
| Tofu Chilli **Low Fat** | Lorraine Fitzmaurice p. 239 | | 2 | | 1½ | |
| Turbot, Red Pepper Escabeche, Virgin Olive Oil and Basil | Ross Lewis, p. 210 | | 1½ | | 4½ | |
| Tuscan Lemon Chicken with Provencal Couscous | Paul Flynn, p. 152 | 1 | 2 | | 5 | |

## DESSERTS

| Recipe | Chef/ Page Number | Fruit Portions | Vegetable Portions | Number of Potatoes | Protein Exchanges | Dairy Product Exchanges |
|---|---|---|---|---|---|---|
| Apple and Berry Strudel | Derry Clarke, p. 62 | ½ | | | | |
| Apple Crumble Ice Cream | Louise Lennox, p. 278 | ½ | | | | ½ |

## DESSERTS

| Recipe | Chef/ Page Number | Fruit Portions | Vegetable Portions | Number of Potatoes | Protein Exchanges | Dairy Product Exchanges |
|---|---|---|---|---|---|---|
| Baked Plums with Blueberries and Orange and Vanilla Meringues **Low Fat** | Paula McIntyre, p. 163 | 2 | | | | |
| Berry Frozen Yoghurt **Low Fat** | Clodagh McKenna, p. 47 | 1 | | | | 1 |
| Blackcurrant Fool with Orange Sponge Fingers | Denis Cotter, p. 229 | 2 | | | | |
| Blueberry Cheesecake | Noel McMeel, p. 131 | ½ | | | | |
| Bread and Butter Pudding | Kevin Dundon, p. 97 | ½ | | | ½ | |
| Caramelised Pear Crêpe with Vanilla Ice Cream | Oliver Dunne, p. 139 | 1 | | | | ½ |
| Carrot and Pineapple Loaf | Catherine Leyden, p. 28 | ½ | ½ | | | |
| Carrot Cake | Lorraine Fitzmaurice, p. 240 | | ½ | | | |
| Double-Crust Apple Pie | Georgina Campbell, p. 86 | 1 | | | | |
| Easy Baked Pears **Low Fat** | Paula Mee, p. 171 | 1½ | | | | |
| Fluffy American Pancakes | Peter Merrigan, p. 179 | ½ | | | | |
| Lemon Crème Caramel with Mango Puree | Ross Lewis, p. 212 | 1 | | | ½ | |
| Lemon Meringue Pie | Claire Nash, p. 38 | ½ | | | 1 | |
| Lemon Tart | Leylie Hayes, p. 105 | ½ | | | 1 | |
| Mini Meringues with Mango and Lime Cream | Catherine Fulvio, p. 17 | ½ | | | | |
| Orange Cake with Raspberry Oil | Liz Moore, p. 113 | ½ | | | | |
| Orange Syrup Polenta Slice | Tony Keogh, p. 254 | ½ | | | | |

## DESSERTS

| Recipe | Chef/ Page Number | Fruit Portions | Vegetable Portions | Number of Potatoes | Protein Exchanges | Dairy Product Exchanges |
|---|---|---|---|---|---|---|
| Passion Fruit Soufflé | David McCann, p. 55 | 1½ | | | 1 | |
| Passion Fruit Tart | Neven Maguire, p. 122 | ½ | | | ½ | |
| Pavlova with Passion fruit and Kiwi | Rachel Allen, p. 187 | ½ | | | | |
| Pear and Apple Crumble | Domini Kemp, p. 71 | 1 | | | | |
| Pear, Pomegranate and Maple Tarte Tatin | Denis Cotter, p. 230 | 1½ | | | | |
| Plum and Cherry Clafoutis | Tony Keogh, p. 257 | 2 | | | 1 | |
| Profiteroles | Catherine Leyden p. 23 | | | | ½ | |
| Quick and Easy Fresh Berry Ice Cream | Eugene McSweeney, p. 79 | ½ | | | | ½ |
| Raspberry and Passion fruit Mousse | Louise Lennox, p. 277 | 1 | | | ½ | |
| Roast Peaches or Nectarines with Honey **Low Fat** | Rory O'Connell, p. 205 | 1 | | | | |
| Shortbread | Catherine Leyden, p. 25 | | | | | |
| Sticky Toffee Pudding with Caramel Sauce and Fresh Cream | Brian Fallon, p. 9 | | | | | |
| Strawberry and Cream Sponge | Catherine Leyden, p. 31 | ½ | | | ½ | |
| Tarte Tatin | Paul Flynn, p. 155 | 1 | | | | |
| Vanilla Crème Brûlée | Patrick McLarnon, p. 147 | | | | ½ | |
| Vanilla Pannacotta with Poached Pears | Richie Wilson, p. 196 | 1½ | | | | ½ |

Chefs

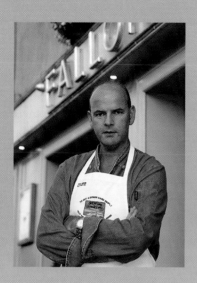

# Brian Fallon

*Brian Fallon*

## Cooking is in the Blood

There was never any doubt that Brian Fallon would become a chef. Coming from a family that is credited with being the first to offer good 'pub grub' in Ireland, Brian knew from an early age that cooking was in his blood. "I was born into the business. My parents ran the Red House, which was between Naas and Newbridge, and in 1977 the whole family moved there."

After school Brian headed off to work in Germany for a year. "After Germany, I worked in America and Australia, so in 1988 I was glad to come home and run the Red House when my parents retired." Brian continued to build his reputation at the Red House until 2004. "Unfortunately, the restaurant caught fire and we had to close. It was then that we opened Fallon's Bar and Café in Kilcullen. Originally we just wanted to have a place to work while the Red House was rebuilt, but the restaurant became so popular in its present location that we decided to stay and do a bit of a revamp."

Brian can trace his love of good food back to his childhood at the Red House. "My mother was a great cook and she inspired me to want to work in the kitchen. In terms of learning the basics, I worked with a wonderful chef called Willie Ryan. Willie was the head chef at the Hibernian Hotel in Dublin, and he was an old-school Escoffier chef and a great teacher. Then in Australia I worked with one of the Roux brothers, so I learned different styles and techniques. But deep down inside I still love nothing better than honest home cooking."

Having worked with some great chefs, Brian likes to keep his food as simple as possible. "I am passionate about flavours and ingredients. My main aim is to support our local producers. I don't want to buy food that has been travelling on the high seas or has been in a cold storage unit for months."

As an active member of Good Food Ireland, Fallon's Bar and Café wants to know exactly where their ingredients have come from. "We are great believers in the whole 'Farm to Fork' ethos of Good Food Ireland. I think it is important not only for the chefs but for the customers to know that the produce on their plate came from a farm less than ten miles from the restaurant and has been handled as little as possible. As a chef, if you are working with good ingredients, you rarely have to do very much to them. Really fresh fish is a good example of 'less is more': simply cooked and served – that's all it needs to be."

At home, Brian applies this philosophy to cooking for his family. "We try to eat fish about three times a week but I also love a good steak. There is nothing better than a 'black and blue' steak from the barbecue, charred on the outside and rare on the inside – I just love it!

"I found working on the recipes for this book quite difficult at times, but the process has made me think about how adding different flavours can work when you can't use the usual ingredients. I must say, I really enjoyed the challenge."

*Fallon Bar & Café, Main Street, Kilcullen, Co. Kildare. Tel: 045 481260; www.fallonb.ie*
*Fallon & Byrne, 2 Exchequer Street, Dublin 2. Tel: 01 4721000; www.fallonandbyrne.com*

* Please note the garnish in the photograph was included for illustration purposes only.

# Tabouli

**Serves 4**

225g (8oz) couscous
220ml (7fl oz) boiling water
3 tbsp extra-virgin olive oil
2 tbsp fresh squeezed lemon juice
2 garlic cloves, finely minced
25g (1oz) fresh mint leaves, coarsely chopped
25g (1oz) fresh coriander, coarsely chopped
25g (1oz) fresh dill, coarsely chopped
60g (2oz) plum tomatoes, seeded and diced
50g (2oz) cucumber, seeded and diced
25g (1oz) spring onions, thinly sliced
A pinch (¼ level tsp) freshly ground black pepper

Place the couscous in a bowl and pour in enough boiling water to just cover the top of the couscous. Let sit until the water has been absorbed and the couscous is softened.

Mix the soaked couscous in a large bowl with olive oil, lemon juice and garlic. Add the chopped mint, coriander and dill. Toss in tomatoes, cucumbers and spring onions. Season with freshly ground pepper. Toss gently but thoroughly and leave to rest for 1 hour at room temperature, covered with clingfilm, to allow the flavours to blend.

To serve, arrange on plates.

 *Per portion* this dish provides 1 portion of vegetables.

*Check your daily allowances to see if you have enough remaining for this dish.*

Brian Fallon

5

# Medallions of Beef with Garlic Butter and Roasted Vegetables

**Serves 4**

**FOR THE ROASTED VEGETABLES**

2 medium onions

½ red pepper, seeded

½ yellow pepper, seeded

100g (3½oz) courgette

2 tbsp olive oil

1 level tsp garlic, crushed

**FOR THE BEEF**

4 x 150g (5oz) medallions of beef

2 tbsp olive oil

90g (3½oz) butter, softened to room temperature

1 garlic clove, crushed

10g (½oz) fresh parsley, chopped

Preheat your oven to 200°C/400°F/Gas 6.

Cut the vegetables into bite-sized chunks and mix together with olive oil and crushed garlic until they are well coated. Place on a baking tray and cook in the hot oven for 30–40 minutes.

To cook the steaks, heat a cast-iron griddle pan (or frying pan) with a metal handle until very hot. Cook the steaks for 5–7 minutes and then transfer the seared steaks to the oven and cook for 10 minutes for well-done, turning the steaks depending on their thickness.

To make the garlic butter, mix the soft butter, crushed garlic and chopped parsley together in a small bowl.

To serve, spoon the roast vegetables on to a plate, place the beef on top (you may want to cut the medallion and serve it in two halves) and finish with a teaspoon of garlic butter. You can serve with rice.

 **Per portion** *this dish provides 2 portions of vegetables and 5 protein exchanges.*

*Check your daily allowances to see if you have enough remaining for this dish.*

# Sticky Toffee Pudding with Caramel Sauce and Fresh Cream

**Serves 8**

50g (2oz) unsalted butter (plus a little extra for greasing)
150g (5oz) soft dark brown sugar
1½ eggs (or one very large egg)
200g (7oz) plain cream flour
¼ level tsp bread soda

**FOR THE CARAMEL SAUCE**
225ml (8fl oz) cream
90g (3½oz) soft dark brown sugar
40g (1¾oz) unsalted butter, roughly chopped

**TO SERVE**
250ml (9fl oz) cream

Preheat the oven to 180°C/350°F/Gas 4.

Mix the butter and sugar together in a large bowl until creamy. Slowly add the eggs.
Sift the flour and bread soda on top and gently fold in with a metal spoon, mixing well.

Grease 8 x 100ml (3½fl oz) dariole moulds. Fill each one to about halfway with the mixture and place them on a baking tray. Bake for 20–25 minutes until risen and cooked through.

To make the caramel sauce, place the sugar and butter in a saucepan (copper if you have one) with half the quantity of cream. Over a medium heat, bring gently to the boil, stirring frequently, until the sugar dissolves. Stir in the remaining cream and return to the boil and then remove from the heat.

When cool enough to handle, trim the peak from each pudding to give a flat surface (saving it to serve as an extra bit on the side).

To serve, tip each pudding out of the mould on to each serving plate, pour some hot caramel sauce over each one and serve with fresh cream.

 *This dessert does not use up any of your daily allowances of fruit, vegetable, potato, protein or dairy.*

# Catherine Fulvio

## Food and Football

Growing up on a farm had a lot to do with Catherine Fulvio's long-term love of good food. At home in Ballyknocken, Co. Wicklow, Catherine's mother decided to open a farm-house bed and breakfast. "I was very young when my mother opened the farm to guests back in the seventies. Back then Irish families spent their holidays at home and many farms took in guests during the summer. So I watched my mother cooking the meals and my father bringing in the milk and the vegetables for the table."

Catherine grew up helping her mother and father with the business. "I would help with the baking or bringing in the potatoes or collecting the herbs; it was a great introduction to good wholesome food." While Catherine's interest in good food continued to grow, college beckoned and, following a degree in German and Irish, Catherine worked in PR and marketing. "I continued to help out at weekends on the farm but it wasn't until my mother died that I decided to come home and take over Ballyknocken House. We completely renovated the house and regraded as a four star guest house." Catherine then converted an empty milking parlour into, the now famous Ballyknocken Cookery School.

With Catherine's love of good food and her Italian husband Claudio, Ballyknocken has gone from strength to strength and, in 2008, Catherine was awarded the Culinary Academy Award for Cookery School of the Year 2007 from the Cordon D'or at a ceremony in Florida.

Having an Italian husband has its advantages when you love good food. "My first holiday with Claudio was pure foodie heaven. We toured Tuscany eating and drinking – it was bliss. In Sicily, where Claudio is from, there are only two subjects that are discussed at the table: food and football. And if Palermo are playing then there is no conversation at all," says Catherine with a laugh.

So is it Italian food first for Catherine? "No not necessarily. I think we are very lucky here in Ireland. We produce wonderful food and wonderful artisan produce, and the quality of the food we produce is exceptional. Italian food is lighter and lends itself to quicker meals. When I cook for the family in Italy they love the Irish meals I prepare for them. I think we can hold our own when it comes to good food."

Catherine loves to keep it simple when it comes to the meals she prepares for her family at home. "My treat after a long day at the cookery school is a nice piece of Wicklow beef with a green salad and a balsamic dressing, nice and simple and full of flavour." And it is with this in mind that Catherine has created her menu for this cookbook. "I was surprised at some of the restrictions and I really hope my recipes will make life easier for those on a renal diet. My advice would be to try to buy organic where you can but always try and buy local. It makes such a difference to know where your food has come from. But most of all enjoy your cooking and your food."

*Ballyknocken House & Cookery School, Glenealy, Ashford, Co Wicklow.*
*Tel: 0404 44627; www.thecookeryschool.ie*

# Chicken Soup

**Serves 4**

2 tsp olive oil
2 onions, finely sliced
2 celery sticks, chopped
2 carrots, peeled and diced
50g (2oz) plain flour
1 litre (1¾ pints) chicken stock (use only 1 suitable stock cube to 1lt water)
450g (1lb) cooked chicken, skinned and shredded
A pinch (¼ level tsp) freshly ground pepper
2 level tbsp fresh parsley, chopped

Heat the oil in a large saucepan and gently fry the onions, celery and carrots until softened. Stir in the flour and cook for 2 minutes.

Gradually stir in the chicken stock and bring to the boil, stirring all the time. Season with pepper and simmer for 10 minutes until the vegetables are tender. Add the cooked shredded chicken and heat through.

Stir in the parsley and serve ladled into warm bowls.

Serve with warm crusty bread.

 *Per portion* *this dish provides 2 portions of vegetables and 5 protein exchanges.*

*If you are on a fluid restriction remember to count this soup as part of your daily intake. Do not use a homemade chicken stock. Ask your dietitian to suggest a suitable stock cube. Note this recipe is high in protein and could be served as a main course.*

*Check your daily allowances to see if you have enough remaining for this dish.*

# Moroccan Lamb Tagine with Lemon Couscous

**Serves 4**

### FOR THE LAMB

1 level tsp ground black pepper

½ level tsp ground cinnamon

½ level tsp ground ginger

½ level tsp ground coriander

3 tbsp water

750g (1¾lb) diced shoulder of lamb, well trimmed

2 tbsp olive oil

1 onion, chopped

1 garlic clove, finely chopped

300ml (10fl oz) vegetable stock (use ½ suitable stock cube to 300ml water)

1 tbsp honey

½ level tsp turmeric

### FOR THE LEMON COUSCOUS

450ml (16fl oz) water

300g (11oz) couscous

Zest and juice of ½ lemon

50ml (2fl oz) extra-virgin olive oil

1 level tbsp fresh flat-leaf parsley, chopped

1 level tbsp fresh coriander, chopped

A pinch (¼ level tsp) freshly ground black pepper

Mix the black pepper, cinnamon, ginger, coriander and turmeric with 3 tablespoons of water to make a marinade for the lamb. Coat the lamb in this marinade, cover with clingfilm and let sit somewhere cool for approximately 1 hour.

While the lamb is marinating, make the couscous. Pour the couscous into a large pot. Heat the water to boiling and pour the liquid over the couscous in a thin, steady stream. Stir in the lemon zest and set aside for 3 minutes, until the grains have swollen and absorbed all the liquid.

Return the couscous to the heat, add the olive oil and lemon juice and cook gently for about 2 minutes, stirring with a fork to fluff up the grains. Take the pan off the heat. Stir in the parsley and coriander. Season to taste with pepper and set aside to keep warm.

Drain the lamb. Heat the olive oil in a frying pan and sauté the lamb until lightly browned. Transfer to a saucepan with a lid (or a tagine, if you own one).

Add the onion to the frying pan that you used to brown the lamb and cook until soft, not brown. Add the garlic and lightly cook. Transfer all to the saucepan (or tagine) with the lamb.

Deglaze the frying pan with a little stock and then pour this and the rest of the stock over the lamb, adding in the marinade spices as well. Bring to the boil. Cover and simmer for approximately 1½ hours or until the lamb is meltingly tender but still holding its shape.

Then add the honey. Keeping the saucepan uncovered, cook for another 10 minutes to reduce and thicken the sauce.

Serve the tagine stew on individual warmed plates or on one large platter to share, with lemon couscous on the side.

 **Per portion** *this dish provides 1 portion of vegetables and 5 protein exchanges.*

*Do not use a homemade vegetable stock. Ask your dietitian to suggest a suitable stock cube.*

*Some of your vegetable allowance has been used to allow the inclusion of vegetable stock in this recipe and therefore we do not recommend that you use it on a regular basis.*

*Check your daily allowances to see if you have enough remaining for this dish.*

# Mini Meringues with Mango and Lime Cream

**Serves 8**

| FOR THE MERINGUE | FOR THE MANGO AND LIME CREAM |
|---|---|
| 5 large egg whites | 600ml (1pt) fresh cream |
| 300g (11oz) caster sugar | 1 level tsp icing sugar |
| 2 level tsp cornflour | Zest and juice of ½ lime (to taste) |
| | 150g (5oz) fresh ripe mango, peeled, stoned and diced |

Preheat the oven to 130°C/250°F/Gas ½.

To make the meringues, draw 8 x 6cm (2¼in) circles on parchment paper, leaving spaces in between each circle. Place the paper on a large baking tray.

Place the egg whites in a large, spotlessly clean, dry bowl (preferably stainless steel or copper). With an electric mixer, whisk the egg whites until they are firm enough to form stiff peaks. Sieve the caster sugar with the cornflour and whisk into the mixture a tablespoon at a time, whisking until the sugar is dissolved.

Spread a 2cm (¾in) layer of meringue evenly over the circles drawn on the parchment paper. To create an edge for the sides of your meringue nests, place the mixture into a piping bag fitted with a plain or star-shaped nozzle and pipe, or alternatively spoon, the mixture around the edges of each circle.

Place the meringues in the oven and bake for about 1½ hours or until the meringue is crisp and just very lightly coloured.

To make the mango and lime cream, whip the cream and fold in the icing sugar and lime zest. Add a little lime juice to taste until you are happy with the sweet/sour flavour.

To serve, fill the meringue nests with lime cream and top with diced mango.

 **Per portion** this dessert provides ½ a portion of fruit.

*Check your daily allowances to see if you have enough remaining for this dessert.*

* Please note the garnish of mint in the photograph was included for illustration purposes only.

Catherine Leyden

# Catherine Leyden

## Queen of Baking

Baking for some is more that just making something good to eat. The very act of baking is more than merely adding ingredients into a bowl. For Catherine Leyden, it was at her grandmother's side that her passion for baking took hold. "I remember watching my grandmother weighing the flour and breaking the eggs – it looked like magic to me."

Being the eldest of ten children, Catherine remembers baking scones, bread and cakes as a natural part of her day. "At school I loved home economics, and when I left school I wanted not only to cook and bake but to teach as well. Then one day I answered an ad from Odlums in one of the newspapers. The ad said that Odlums was looking for a 'home economist and lady demonstrator'. It sounded like my dream job so I applied, and thirty-four years later I am still with the company!"

As the job description detailed, Catherine was not only to be responsible for testing recipes but also for showing people how to make them. "Things have changed a lot in my thirty-four years. I started off compiling recipes but I also had the opportunity to travel around the country giving demonstrations to different groups. In the beginning it was mainly the Irish Countrywomen's Association (ICA) groups and smaller community groups in parish halls and schools. Then TV3 came along and a new opportunity arose."

Having promoted Odlums products around the country for all those years, Catherine didn't find the move to TV too daunting. "Giving a demonstration on television is no different from standing in front of a group in a parish hall, although on TV the viewers miss out on the wonderful smells and tastes of it all."

On TV3's *Ireland AM*, Catherine is known as the "Queen of Baking" but her popularity has also crossed the Atlantic, where she has shared some of her recipes with viewers in the USA. "I appeared on *The Martha Stewart Show* for a St Patrick's Day special, which was great fun."

For Catherine, baking is more than just another part of cooking. "Baking to me is an eternal act; I find baking very therapeutic. It's all about the smell, the anticipation and then the taste. My day wouldn't be the same without baking." Catherine has some favourites when it comes to baking at home. "I love to make quiches and pies but what I really have a passion for is baking bread with yeast. "Sadly, I think over the years baking in Ireland has changed a lot. Back when I started, especially in rural Ireland, brown bread would be baked every morning. Now, with so many people living frenetic city lives, baking has become something only done for a special occasion. Today, a lot of younger people just don't have baking skills because these skills have not been passed on."

When Catherine first saw the list of approved ingredients for this book, she admits she was a little daunted. "At first I struggled a bit, but that's the beauty about baking: you can adapt ingredients and still get great results."

*Odlums Recipes, c/o Shamrock Foods Ltd., Merrywell Industrial Estate, Ballymount, Dublin 12. Tel: 01 4051500   www.odlums.ie*

# High Fibre Brown Soda Bread

**Makes 15 thin slices**

400g (14oz) coarse wholemeal flour
1 tbsp (15g) brown sugar
A pinch (¼ level tsp) salt
1 level tsp bread soda, sieved
1 tbsp vegetable oil, plus extra for greasing
300ml (½pt) milk
125g (4½oz) natural yoghurt

1 x 900g (2lb) loaf tin

Preheat oven to 200°C/400°F/Gas 6. Grease a 900g (2lb) loaf tin.

Put wholemeal flour, sugar, salt and bread soda into a mixing bowl and mix well together.
Make a well in the centre and add the oil, milk and yoghurt and stir until well blended.
The mixture will be quite wet.

Transfer to the prepared tin, make a cut down the centre and bake for 45 minutes. To check
if the bread is fully baked, tap the loaf on the base. If it is done it will make a hollow sound.

Wrap in a clean tea towel and allow to cool. The bread cuts better if left until the next day.
Cut into slices before serving.

*Each thin slice* of bread has the equivalent of 30ml milk. If you have a daily
allowance of dairy products, this needs to be taken from your daily allowance.

*This soda bread is higher in phosphate and potassium than white bread therefore
if you are on a phosphate or potassium restriction you need to discuss this recipe
with your dietitian.*

# White Scones

**Serves 6**

225g (8oz) plain flour, plus extra for dusting
1 level tsp bread soda
25g (1oz) caster sugar (optional)
25g (1oz) margarine
150ml (¼pt) buttermilk

Preheat oven to 220°C/425°F/Gas 7. Flour a baking sheet and leave it in the oven to preheat.

Sieve the flour, bread soda and sugar (if using) into a bowl. Rub in the margarine, using the tips of the fingers. Add the buttermilk and mix to make a soft dough.

Turn the dough on to a lightly floured board and knead, if necessary, to remove any cracks. Roll out lightly to 2.5cm (1in) thickness and cut into scones with a 5cm (2in) cutter, dipped in flour.

Place the scones on the floured pre-heated baking sheet and bake for 10–12 minutes until well risen and nicely browned.

Cool on a wire rack. Cut open to serve.

 *Each scone has the equivalent of 25ml milk. If you have a daily allowance of dairy products, this needs to be taken from your daily allowance.*

# Profiteroles

**Serves 5 (allow 2 profiteroles per portion)**

150ml (¼pt) water
50g (2oz) margarine, plus extra for greasing
65g (2½oz) strong white flour, sieved
A pinch (¼ level tsp) salt
2 eggs, beaten
Icing sugar, to dust

**FOR THE FILLING**
300ml (½pt) fresh cream, whipped

Preheat oven to 200°C/400°F/Gas 6. Line a baking tin with greaseproof paper.

Place water and margarine into a saucepan over a low heat until margarine melts. Bring to a brisk boil. Reduce heat and add sieved flour and salt. Stir briskly until mixture forms a soft dough and leaves sides of saucepan. Remove from heat and allow to cool.

Gradually add the eggs and beat until mixture is smooth and shiny. Drop a tablespoon of dough about 7.5cm (3in) apart on to a greased baking sheet, making 10.

Bake in the pre-heated oven for 20 minutes or until puffed up and golden. Remove from oven and slit along one side. Cool on a wire rack.

When the profiteroles are cold, whip the cream in a bowl until soft peaks form, then use to fill the profiteroles. Serve dusted with icing sugar.

**Per portion** *this dessert provides ½ a protein exchange.*

*While you don't usually think of desserts as having a lot of protein – this recipe has approximately ½ an egg per portion and therefore it has been counted in the protein allowances for this recipe.*

*Check your daily allowance to see if you have enough remaining for this dessert.*

# Shortbread

**Makes 8 wedges**

125g (4oz) butter, at room temperature, plus extra for greasing
50g (2oz) caster sugar
125g (4oz) plain flour
50g (2oz) cornflour

1 x 18cm (7in) round sandwich tin

Preheat oven to 160°C/325°F/Gas 3. Grease an 18cm (7in) round sandwich tin.

Beat butter and sugar together in a bowl until smooth using a wooden spoon or electric mixer. Add the flour and the cornflour and mix gently until a dough is formed. Use fingertips to form dough into a ball and lightly knead, if necessary. Press dough into the greased tin. Prick around top of dough with a fork. Bake in oven for about 20 minutes or until very pale in colour.

Allow to 'set' in tin for 5 minutes, mark out wedges with a sharp knife and then transfer to a wire rack to cool. As soon as shortbread is cold, store in an airtight tin. Arrange on a plate to serve.

*To make biscuits, roll out mixture and cut out rounds using a 7cm (3in) cutter shape. For fingers, press dough into an 18cm (7in) square tin and cut into fingers after baking.*

*This recipe does not use up any of your daily allowances of fruit, vegetable, potato, protein or dairy.*

# Cheese, Onion and Tomato Quiche

**Serves 4**

**FOR THE PASTRY FLAN CASE**

175g (6oz) plain flour, plus extra for dusting
75g (3oz) margarine
A little cold water

**FOR THE FILLING**

1 small onion, finely chopped
50g (2oz) Cheddar cheese, made with
    pasteurised milk, grated
130g (4½oz) tomatoes, sliced
300ml (½pt) milk
2 eggs
A pinch (¼ level tsp) freshly ground black pepper

**FOR THE SALAD**

100g (3½oz) mixed salad leaves,
    freshly washed (may include butterhead,
    boston, bibb, webb, cos, romaine, iceberg,
    red leaf and rocket. Avoid spinach leaves.)
3 tbsp extra-virgin olive oil
2 tsp balsamic vinegar
A pinch (¼ level tsp) freshly ground black pepper

Pre-heat oven to 190°C/375°F/Gas 5.

Sieve the flour into a bowl and coarsely rub in the margarine. Add sufficient cold water to make a soft dough. Roll out the dough on a floured surface to about 5mm (¼in) thickness.

Line a 23cm (9in) flan dish with the pastry, cutting off any excess pastry around the edges. Place onion and cheese into the flan case. Arrange tomato slices on top.

Beat eggs and milk together and add pepper to season. Pour gently into flan case. Bake in the oven for about 30 minutes or until golden brown and set firm.

Serve hot or cold with a little salad at the side.

***Per portion*** *this dish provides 1½ portions of vegetables, ½ a protein exchange and 1 dairy exchange.*

*Check your daily allowances to see if you have enough remaining for this dish.*

# Carrot and Pineapple Loaf

**Makes 12 slices**

175g (6oz) plain flour
125g (4oz) sugar
1 level tsp bread soda
1 level tsp cinnamon
125g (4oz) grated carrot
1 x 432g tin crushed pineapple, tinned in its own juice, drained well (drained weight 240g)
1 egg
3 tbsp sunflower oil
1 tsp vanilla essence

Preheat oven to 180°C/350°F/Gas 4. Lightly grease a 900g (2lb) loaf tin.

Put the flour, sugar, sieved bread soda and cinnamon into a mixing bowl. Stir in the carrot and pineapple. Beat egg, oil and vanilla essence together and add to the dry ingredients. Beat until ingredients are all well combined.

Transfer to the prepared tin and bake for about 1 to 1½ hours until firm to the touch. When you insert a knife into the centre of the loaf it should come out clean when it is cooked through.

Turn on to a wire rack to cool.

 *Two slices of this loaf provide ½ a portion of fruit and ½ a portion of vegetables.*

*Check your daily allowances to see if you have enough remaining for two slices of this loaf.*

# Strawberry and Cream Sponge

**Serves 6**

Butter, for greasing
3 eggs, separated
A pinch (¼ level tsp) salt
75g (3oz) caster sugar
75g (3oz) plain flour
¼ tsp vanilla essence (optional)

2 x 18cm (7in) sandwich tins

**FOR THE FILLING**
12 fresh strawberries (approx. 145g/5oz),
  hulled and sliced in half
150ml (¼pt) cream
Icing sugar, to dust

Preheat oven to 200°C/400°F/Gas 6. Grease and base line two 18cm (7in) sandwich tins with greaseproof paper.

Place the three egg whites and the salt in a large, clean, dry mixing bowl. Stiffly beat until mixture is dry looking in appearance. Next, add the sugar and beat for a few seconds; then add the egg yolks and beat until mixture thickens and the trail of the beaters is visible. Finally, sieve in the flour and fold it into the thick mixture using a large metal spoon. To fold, just cut through the mixture, over and over, with the metal spoon until all the flour is blended in. Never beat the mixture, as that will beat out all the air!

Fold the vanilla essence (if you are using it) into the sponge mixture, then transfer the mixture to the prepared tins and bake for 15 minutes, until the sponge is risen and springs back when gently touched. Turn on to a wire rack, remove the lining paper and allow to cool.

Whip the cream until soft peaks form. When the sponges are cold, cover one sponge with whipped cream and top with fresh strawberries. Place the other sponge on top, then dust with icing sugar. Cut into slices to serve.

 ***Per portion*** *this dessert provides ½ a portion of fruit and ½ a protein exchange.*

*While you don't usually think of a cake having a lot of protein, this recipe has ½ an egg per portion and therefore it has been counted in the protein allowances for this recipe.*

*Check your daily allowances to see if you have enough remaining for this dessert.*

Catherine Leyden

# Claire Nash

## *Life is Too Short to Eat Bad Food*

A disciple of the legendary Myrtle Allen and the Ballymaloe experience, Claire Nash knows good food. "I started with Myrtle Allen when I was thirteen years old, washing dishes in the hotel. She was the person who inspired my passion for food. The Ballymaloe ethos was all about sourcing seasonal ingredients and cooking them simply to allow the flavour to shine, and that is what I love about food."

After school, Claire decided to do a catering course at Cathal Brugha Street in Dublin and from there moved on to study business at Trinity College. "I knew that if I wanted to run my own business some day, then I would have to know as much about economics as I do about food and ingredients."

When Claire graduated, she decided to look for work in America. "I took a job in a country club in Atlanta, Georgia. It was there that I learned about working with people and about the day-to-day running of a business. When I came home in early 1990, I wanted to open my own restaurant – and here I am nineteen years later!"

Claire knows that her business success is due to her core ethos regarding good food.

"When it comes to good food, maintaining standards is key and paying constant attention to the small details. At Nash 19, we source our food from local suppliers. We have quite a simple formula – our food is improving all the time and, as members of Good Food Ireland, we want to champion Irish food, simply cooked."

At home, Claire loves to bake. "I bake bread every Saturday morning. I don't think there is anything better than the smell of bread baking. Homemade Irish soda bread is my favourite. I love shopping for my food and I only buy what I need that day. I never decide what I want until I get to the shop or the market and then I choose what looks good. Also, it's great to talk to a butcher or a grower at the farmers' market and ask what they recommend. Your butcher will give you all the experience he or she has learned over the years and will show you other cuts of meat that you might not have used before."

Claire enjoyed the challenge we set her for this book. "It was a very interesting project and one that made us rethink a lot of what we would do as a matter of course in our everyday cooking. One thing that I feel is most important is that you source your ingredients from producers who care about their food. Eat as seasonally as you can – it makes such a difference when the food you eat has travelled from a farm in your area.

"Don't over-buy: get only what you need for that meal and then the food will be fresh and full of flavour. The most important thing is to enjoy your cooking and enjoy the food you like. Life is too short to eat bad food."

*Nash 19, Princes Street, Cork city. Tel: 021 4270880; www.nash19.com*

# Cod and Salmon Tofu Cakes

**Serves 8**

2 x 160g (5½oz) blocks of tofu, cut into small pieces

300g (10oz) fresh cod, skin and bones removed
and cut into small pieces

300g (10oz) fresh salmon, skin and bones removed
and cut into small pieces

30g (1oz) red chillis, seeded and finely diced

4 level tsp fresh ginger, peeled and grated

2–3 spring onions, finely chopped

A pinch (¼ level tsp) cracked black pepper

Olive oil, for deep frying

150g (5oz) salad leaves, to serve (may include butterhead, boston, bibb, webb, cos,
romaine, iceberg, red leaf and rocket. Avoid spinach leaves.)

3 tbsp extra-virgin olive oil

1 tsp balsamic vinegar

A pinch (¼ level tsp) freshly ground black pepper

**FOR THE BREADCRUMBS**

50g (2oz) plain flour

2 eggs

100g (4oz) dried breadcrumbs

Mix the cod, salmon and tofu together well with a wooden spoon. Add the finely diced chilli, ginger and spring onions. Season with cracked black pepper. Shape the mixture into 8 small cakes and place on a large plate. Cover and chill in the fridge for 10 minutes.

To crumb the fishcakes first beat the eggs. Lay out two plates with the flour on one and the breadcrumbs on the other. Dip the fishcakes first in the flour, then coat in the egg mixture and finally cover with breadcrumbs. Set aside.

Fill a deep pan or wok with 2 inches of olive oil and heat. Once the oil has come up to temperature, deep-fry the fishcakes (3 or 4 at a time, depending on the size of your pan) for 4–5 minutes until golden brown and hot throughout. Or you could bake them in a moderate oven (preheated to 180°C/350°F/Gas 4) for about 15 minutes.

To prepare the salad, wash the salad leaves. Add the oil, vinegar and pepper into a bowl and mix well with a fork. Add the salad leaves and toss to coat.

Serve each cod and salmon tofu cake with a little salad on the side.

*Per portion* this dish provides ½ a portion of vegetables and 3 protein exchanges.

*Check your daily allowances to see if you have enough remaining for this dish.*

35

# Fillet of Pork Frascati with Basmati Rice

**Serves 6**

600g (1¼lb) pork steak, sliced into chunks
A pinch (¼ level tsp) white pepper
2 tbsp olive oil
1 Spanish onion, finely sliced
200g (7oz) peppers, red and/or yellow (not green),
    deseeded and sliced
1 clove of garlic, finely chopped
1½ tbsp brandy

570ml (1pt) cream
2 bay leaves
1 level tbsp (7g) ground paprika
Zest and juice of 1 lemon

**FOR THE BASMATI RICE**
350g (12oz) basmati rice
350ml (12fl oz) water

Season the strips of pork with the white pepper. Heat half the olive oil in a large frying pan and, when oil is beginning to smoke, add the pork to the pan to fry for a minute or two to seal in the flavours. Remove the pan from the heat and set aside.

In a medium-sized pot, heat the rest of the olive oil and sauté the onions, mixed peppers and garlic. Add the brandy to deglaze the pot (pick up all the cooking juices). Next add the cream and let the sauce simmer gently for about 15 minutes until the amount of liquid is reduced by a third. Your sauce will have thickened slightly at this point.

Add the seared pork strips and their cooking juices and bay leaves to the pot and allow to simmer gently for about 20–30 minutes until pork is tender and fully cooked. Finally season with paprika and juice and zest of the lemon.

To make lovely fluffy basmati rice, wash the rice in several changes of cold water, then leave to soak for about 30 minutes in fresh cold water. Drain the rice and put into a medium saucepan. Add the water, bring to the boil and cover with a tight-fitting lid. Turn the heat to the lowest setting and leave the rice to cook for 10 minutes before turning off the heat. Don't lift the lid; just leave the rice to continue cooking in its own steam for about 5 minutes until you're ready to serve. It is important that you do not lift the lid and allow the steam to escape as this steam will continue to cook the rice for the last 5 minutes as it stands. The rice should have absorbed all the water and will just need fluffing up with a fork.
To serve, divide the rice among warm plates and spoon over the fillet of pork Frascati.

* Please note the garnish in the photograph was included for illustration purposes only.

 **Per portion** *this dish provides 1 portion of vegetables, 3 protein exchanges and ¼ a dairy exchange.*

*As there is a large amount of cream (which is made from milk) in the recipe we have counted it as ¼ of a dairy exchange (see allowances above).*

*Check your daily allowances to see if you have enough remaining for this dish.*

# Lemon Meringue Pie

**Serves 8**

**FOR THE PASTRY**
175g (6oz) plain flour,
   plus extra for dusting
50g (2oz) butter
30g (1¼oz) caster sugar
1 egg
A little cold water, if necessary

**FOR THE MERINGUE TOPPING**
6 egg whites
300g (11oz) caster sugar

**FOR THE LEMON CURD**
Zest and juice of 4 lemons
3½ level tbsp cornflour
A little water

6 egg yolks (reserve egg whites for meringue mixture)
100g (3½oz) caster sugar
100g (3½oz) butter, at room temperature

To prepare the pastry, preheat oven to 180°C/350°F/Gas 4. Sift the flour into a bowl and rub in the butter until the mixture resembles fine breadcrumbs. Stir in the caster sugar, then add the eggs and mix to form a dough, add a little cold water if necessary. Wrap in clingfilm and leave to rest in the fridge for one hour. This can be left in the fridge overnight.

Roll out the dough on a lightly floured work surface and use to line a deep 23cm (9in) loose-bottomed flan tin. To bake blind, cover the pastry with greaseproof paper and fill with baking beans (either ceramic ones or any raw dried beans, which you can reuse for baking blind). Bake in the oven for 20 minutes. Remove the beans and greaseproof paper and return the pastry case to the oven for 5–10 minutes, until very lightly coloured. (After removing the beans and paper, you could brush the partly cooked pastry with lightly beaten egg white before returning it to the oven. This helps to form a seal and keeps the pastry crisp when you add the filling.) Reduce the oven temperature to 150°C/300°F/Gas 2.

To make the lemon curd filling, in a small saucepan bring the lemon juice to the boil. In a large bowl, dissolve the cornflour in a little water and then pour the hot lemon juice over the cornflour mixture and beat until smooth. Add egg yolks, sugar and butter and blend well. Place mixture into a large pan and cook over medium heat until thick, then add the lemon zest. Pour the lemon curd mixture into the pastry-lined flan case and set aside to cool slightly.

To make the meringue topping, in a clean, dry bowl whisk egg whites and sugar together until they form stiff peaks. Place the stiff egg white mixture into a piping bag and pipe it out evenly to cover the lemon curd mixture. Bake in the oven for about 35–45 minutes until the meringue is crisp on the outside and soft and marshmallow-like underneath.

 You can freeze this lemon meringue pie.

**Per portion** this dessert provides ½ a portion of fruit and 1 protein exchange.

*While you don't usually think of desserts as having a lot of protein, this recipe has approximately 1 egg per portion and therefore it has been counted in the protein allowances for this recipe.*

*Check your daily allowances to see if you have enough remaining for this dessert.*

Claire Nash

39

# Clodagh McKenna

Clodagh McKenna

## *From Farmers' Markets to Food Hero*

After graduating from university in New York, Clodagh McKenna wanted to start her own business. She knew she wanted to work with food and, on returning home to Ireland, decided to enroll at the Ballymaloe Cookery School. "I did the course purely for business reasons. I knew I wanted to work with food but never really saw myself in the kitchen, so to speak."

Like many before her, though, when Clodagh finished her year's training, all she wanted to do was get to work in a kitchen as soon as possible. "I was thrilled to get a job working as a chef at Ballymaloe House, where I stayed for over three years. Then another opportunity arose to set up farmers' markets around the country."

To start with, Clodagh couldn't quite drag herself away from her life in the kitchen. "I started by taking a stall at the Midleton Farmers' Market in East Cork. I set up a commercial kitchen where I made terrines, pâtés and chutneys and sold them at the markets."

It was at the farmers' markets that Clodagh first became involved with television. "Rick Stein was filming his *Food Heroes* TV series and he asked me to help with the research for the Irish section." But it wasn't just behind the camera that Clodagh was working. "I did a small piece for Rick when he was over in Ireland filming and it snowballed from there."

Soon Clodagh McKenna became a household name both in Ireland and the UK. "I published my first book, *The Irish Farmers' Market Cookbook...* and the rest, as they say, is history."

Now she has a new seafood cookbook out and has presented countless cookery programmes on TV herself. "I absolutely adore food and cooking. I am really lucky to be working at something I feel so passionate about.

"I love eating local food. If I am in West Cork, I like food from that area. I always cook with whatever is fresh and seasonal and from the region; I would say that, for me, this is the most important element in eating well." Clodagh lived in Italy for a number of years but has returned now to live in Ireland.

Here at home, Clodagh has seen a real change in the way we look at food and eating. "In Italy, good food is part of everyone's day – good food is something that brings people together, and I believe that we are beginning to sow those seeds now in Ireland as well. I think the Irish talk more about good food these days, and more and more people are trying different types of food, growing their own fruit and vegetables and supporting their local producers by buying at farmers' markets.

"To prepare my recipes in this book, look for vegetables that are in season. When you eat seasonally, you are getting the best nutrients from your food – and if your food hasn't travelled thousands of miles to get to you, then you will taste the difference. I hope that you will have fun cooking my recipes!"

*www.clodaghmckenna.com*

# Cottage Cheese, Pomegranate and Mint Bruschetta

**Serves 4**

200g (7oz) cottage cheese, made with pasteurised milk, strained
½ pomegranate (10g), seeds only
Juice of half a lemon
4 slices sourdough bread
2 level tbsp fresh mint, finely chopped
3 tbsp extra-virgin olive oil
A pinch (¼ level tsp) freshly ground black pepper

Place the cottage cheese, pomegranate seeds and lemon juice into a bowl and mix together. Toast the sourdough slices, in the toaster or under a hot grill, for 2 minutes either side, until golden brown. Stir the mint into the cheese mixture, then season to taste with the ground black pepper. Add 2 tablespoons of really good olive oil and mix through.

To serve, drizzle the sourdough toast with the remaining olive oil and top with a generous spoonful of the cheese mixture on each piece of bread. Arrange on individual plates or serve on one large platter.

 **Per portion** *this dish provides ½ a portion of fruit and 1 dairy exchange.*

*Check your daily allowances to see if you have enough remaining for this dish.*

# Tarragon Plaice En Papillote served with Julienne Vegetables and Chive Mash

**Serves 4**

**FOR THE CHIVE MASH**

800g (1¾lb) potatoes, Kerrs Pink or Maris Piper are both good for mashing
125ml (4fl oz) milk
25g (1oz) butter
2 level tbsp fresh chives, finely chopped (or you could use an equal quantity of spring onion)
A pinch (¼ level tsp) freshly ground black pepper

**FOR THE TARRAGON PLAICE EN PAPILLOTE**

4 plaice fillets (approx. 150g (5oz) each)
8 level tbsp double cream
3 level tbsp fresh tarragon, chopped
A pinch (¼ level tsp) freshly ground black pepper
Juice of 2 lemons

**FOR THE JULIENNE VEGETABLES**

160g (5½oz) carrots, peeled
160g (5½oz) leeks, trimmed
100g (3½oz) courgettes, trimmed
100g (3½oz) butter

Prepare 4 rectangles of greaseproof paper, each about 15 x 20cm (6 x 8in) in size.

To prepare the mash, peel and dice the potatoes into 1cm (½in) cubes. Bring to the boil in 10 times their volume of water (see p. 282). Cook until potatoes are soft. While the potatoes are cooking, gently warm the milk in a small pan. When potatoes are cooked, drain and return to the warm pan. As you mash the potatoes, add in the warm milk in stages to make the mash nice and creamy. Finally add in the butter, let it melt and mix well and then add in the chopped chives (or spring onion). Season with black pepper. Cover the pot of mash with tinfoil and a tight lid to keep it warm.

Meanwhile, prepare the fish. Preheat oven to 200°C/400°F/Gas 6. Place a fillet of plaice in the middle of each sheet of greaseproof paper. Pour two tablespoons of double cream on

top of each one and season with a sprinkle of pepper. Scatter the tarragon over the fillets. Fold the edges of the greaseproof paper together to create a small, sealed parcel (it will look a little like a mini tent). Place your *en papillote* (meaning cooked in parchment) parcels of fish into the oven to bake for 12 minutes.

While the fish is cooking prepare the julienne vegetables by slicing the vegetables into very thin match stick strips. Place a frying pan over a medium heat and melt the butter. Stir in the vegetables and sauté for 10 minutes.

To serve, place the fish on the plate and top with the julienne vegetables; pour the juices from the parcel over each piece of fish. Serve with chive mash on the side.

 **Per portion** *this dish provides 2 portions of vegetables, 2 potatoes (chive mash) and 3 protein exchanges.*

*If you have a daily allowance of dairy products, please note that there is milk in this recipe, which needs to be taken from your allowance.*

*Check your daily allowances to see if you have enough remaining for this dish.*

Clodagh McKenna

# Berry Frozen Yoghurt

**Serves 4**

275g (10oz) mixed frozen berries 70g (2½oz) each of redcurrants, blackberries, raspberries and strawberries or you could use just 275g (10oz) of a single berry)
2 tbsp honey
450g (1lb) natural yoghurt, chilled

Take the frozen fruit out of the freezer, place in a food processor and blend for 10 seconds, then add the honey and yoghurt and blend until smooth. Transfer to an airtight container and put back in the freezer for an hour. If you don't have a food processor you can mash the fruit with a fork then fold into the yoghurt and honey.

To serve, scoop the frozen berry yoghurt into bowls or glasses as you would ice cream.

*Per portion* *this dessert provides 1 portion of fruit and 1 dairy exchange.*

*Check your daily allowances to see if you have enough remaining for this dessert.*

David McCann

# David McCann

## A Chance Meeting

A chance meeting on a country road set the wheels in motion for David McCann, and from then on he knew that the life of a chef was for him. "My father was with the Gardaí and he was stationed in Clontarf. One evening, when we were travelling home to Dundalk, he gave a guy a lift. He was a chef, and by the end of the journey I had decided that cooking was for me."

After school, David applied to CERT and headed off to catering college. "I was completely naïve; after my first placement, in a hotel in Dundalk, I decided that I would finish up the year and then get out as quickly as I could because this was not for me."

After that momentous decision, David was ready to pack his bags and put away the chef's whites for good. "For some reason, and I don't know what that was, I decided to stay put for another year. This turned out to be the most important year of my life. I really got into the course in second year and my second placement was at Dublin's landmark Shelbourne Hotel."

The Shelbourne changed everything for David. "I knew I had made the right choice.

I enjoyed the Shelbourne and I met Kevin Thornton, who had just returned from Canada. From then on, I always worked with people who were really passionate about their profession and about good food."

David then spent nine years cooking in London before returning home to work at the renowned Arbutus Lodge Hotel in Cork. "I wanted to work in hotels; I prefer hotels to restaurants because of the variety of the work. So, for the last fourteen years I have been very happy here in Dromoland Castle."

David describes his background in food as steeped in the classical tradition. "Classical cooking is the basis for my cooking, but I would also say that my food is influenced by what is going on around me. At the moment, we have two chefs from Sri Lanka who came to work with me from Le Gavroche in London. They have introduced me to new ingredients and spices, which is fantastic. Sourcing the best ingredients comes first, whether you are cooking at Dromoland Castle or at home."

Family time is very important for David. "At home, my family favourites are risotto and curries. I love simple, tasty food, using good ingredients."

David found the list of ingredients from the book very interesting. "I found the challenge a great help to me, even in the kitchen at Dromoland. At the hotel, we get lots of people with special dietary needs, so we are able to react to whatever is required.

"I must admit that the renal diet is not one we have come across before. When you set out to make my recipes from the book, remember that freshness is the key. You don't have to rely on the big supermarket chains for all your ingredients – go to your local farmers' market and buy from the people who produce the food."

*Dromoland Castle, Newmarket-on-Fergus, Co. Clare. Tel: 061 368144; www.dromoland.ie*

# Risotto with Paprika and Red Pepper

**Serves 4**

600ml (1pt) vegetable stock (use only 1 suitable vegetable stock cube to 600ml water)
80ml (3fl oz) olive oil
50g (2oz) onion, diced
200g (7oz) red pepper, halved, seeded and diced
2 level tsp paprika
250g (9oz) risotto rice
50g (2oz) butter
6 spring onions, chopped
100g (3½oz) Parmesan made with pasteurised milk, freshly grated

Bring the stock to a gentle simmer in a pan. Heat the oil in a wide-bottomed saucepan, add the onion and the pepper and sauté without letting the onion change colour.
Next add in the rice and paprika, and sauté until a light golden colour. Gradually add the stock one ladleful at a time, to the rice, allowing the rice to absorb the liquid before you add the next ladleful, and stirring occasionally. Continue until you have poured in about ¾ of the stock. The rice should be soft. This will take about 15 minutes.

Next add in the butter, spring onions (hold back a little for a garnish) and Parmesan. Finally add more stock – if you like your risotto quite 'wet', add it all and let it simmer just for a further 5 minutes. If you do not like your risotto 'wet' then only add a little more to loosen it up before serving.

Divide the risotto among warm wide-rimmed bowls to serve and garnish with spring onion.

 *Per portion* this dish provides 2 portions of vegetables and 1 dairy exchange.

*Do not use a homemade vegetable stock. Ask your dietitian to suggest a suitable stock cube. Some of your vegetable allowance has been used to allow the inclusion of vegetable stock in this recipe and therefore we do not recommend that you use it on a regular basis.*

*Check your daily allowances to see if you have enough remaining for this dish.*

David McCann

# Roast Pork Steak with Leeks and Savoy Cabbage, Couscous, Curry Emulsion

**Serves 4**

### FOR THE PORK
600g (1¼lb) pork fillet
50g (2oz) plain flour
1 level tsp ground cumin
1 level tsp ground coriander
1 tbsp olive oil

### FOR THE SAUCE (makes 100ml)
1 tbsp olive oil
25g (1oz) onion, chopped
½ garlic clove, crushed
2 level tsp mild curry powder
60g (2½oz) tomatoes, chopped
100ml (4fl oz) chicken stock (use only ¼
    of a suitable chicken stock cube
    to 100ml water)
50g (2oz) Bramley apple, peeled,
    cored and chopped
50ml (2fl oz) crème fraîche

### FOR THE COUSCOUS
200g (7oz) couscous
300ml (10fl oz) chicken stock (use only ½ a
    suitable chicken stock cube to 300ml water)
150g (5oz) onion, diced
100g (3½oz) fresh apple, peeled, cored and diced
50ml (2fl oz) olive oil
1 level tbsp fresh coriander, finely chopped

### FOR THE LEEKS AND CABBAGE
240g (8oz) savoy cabbage
160g (5½oz) leeks
2 tbsp olive oil

Preheat the oven to 180°C/350°F/Gas 4.

Trim the pork of all fat and sinew. Mix all dry ingredients together and rub them well into the skin of the pork. Heat a large frying pan on the hob, add the oil and brown the pork in the pan on all sides. Then remove to the oven to roast for 25 minutes. Remove and allow to rest.

Meanwhile make the sauce. Heat the oil in a heavy-based pot and add the onion and garlic to soften. Now add the curry powder, tomato and apple, reduce the heat and cook lightly for 5 minutes. Add the stock, increase the heat and cook for 8 minutes or until half the liquid has evaporated. Next add the crème fraîche, bring to the boil and simmer for 5 minutes. Remove from the heat and pass the sauce through a fine strainer into a clean pan. Reheat when ready to serve.

To make the couscous, add the stock, onion and apple into a pot and bring it to the boil.

Remove from the heat. Pour in the couscous and cover with clingfilm. When all the stock has been absorbed, stir the olive oil and coriander into the couscous and set aside.

To prepare the cabbage and leeks, remove the outer leaves of cabbage. Break off each leaf of cabbage until the core is exposed. Remove all the main veins from the centre of each leaf. Now cut the cabbage into fine strips. Wash in cold water and drain. Remove the outer leaf on the leeks, cut the leeks down the centre and wash well. With a chopping knife slice the leeks and drain. Boil the cabbage and leeks in 4 times as much water as vegetables until cooked. Drain and run under cold water. Remove any excess water from the vegetables with a tea towel. Then heat the oil in a large pot, add the cabbage and stir-fry until wilted and tender; do not allow the cabbage to colour. Next add the leeks and continue to cook for 2 minutes. Remove from the heat and set aside.

To serve, carve the pork steak and place on the plates with the vegetables and couscous to the side. Then drizzle a little of the sauce around.

 **Per portion** *this dish provides ½ a portion of fruit, 2 portions of vegetables and 4 protein exchanges.*

*Do not use a homemade chicken stock. Ask your dietitian to suggest a suitable stock cube.*

*Check your daily allowances to see if you have enough remaining for this dish.*

# Passion Fruit Soufflé

**Serves 4**

### FOR THE FRUIT PURÉE

200g (7oz) Bramley apples,
    peeled, cored and diced

2 tbsp water

1 level tbsp cornflour

200ml (7fl oz) orange juice

5 passion fruits, juice and pulp scooped out with a spoon

50g (2oz) caster sugar

### FOR THE SOUFFLÉ

Unsalted butter, to grease soufflé
    moulds

Icing sugar, to dust moulds

200g (7oz) egg whites

50g (2oz) caster sugar

200ml passion fruit purée,
    from before

4 x 200ml (7fl oz) soufflé moulds or straight-sided ramekins

To make apple purée, place the Bramley apples in a saucepan with the water, bring to the boil and simmer for 5 minutes or until softened, then blend to a pulp.

Mix the cornflour with a little orange juice in a small glass bowl. To make the rest of the fruit purée, empty the passion fruit juice, pulp and apple pulp into a saucepan, and add in the rest of the orange juice. Add the sugar, bring to the boil and reduce the mixture to about 200ml (7oz), then thicken with the cornflour and orange juice mixture. Allow to cool to room temperature.

Preheat the oven to 180°C/350°F/Gas 4. Butter the soufflé moulds, making sure to butter all the sides of the mould. Now dust the inside of the buttered moulds with icing sugar; shake off excess sugar. To make the soufflé, place the egg whites in a clean dry bowl. Whisk until the whites begin to stiffen, add the sugar and continue to whisk until stiff.

In another bowl, place two-thirds of the apple and passion fruit purée. Add one-third of the egg white and mix well, then add the remainder of the whites and fold in gently. Place some of the remaining fruit purée in the bottom of each mould, half-fill the moulds with egg white mixture, then add another layer of fruit purée and then fill the moulds with the rest of the soufflé mixture. With a palette knife flatten the surface of the soufflé. With the tip of your thumb clean the rim of the mould and also clean the outside of the mould.

Place in the oven for 8 minutes until well-risen and lightly golden. Remove the soufflés from the moulds, set on plates and dust with icing sugar to serve and enjoy!

 **Per portion** this dessert provides 1½ portions of fruit and 1 protein exchange.

*While you don't usually think of desserts as having a lot of protein, this recipe has the equivalent of about 1 egg per portion and therefore it has been counted in the protein allowances for this recipe.*

*Check your daily allowances to see if you have enough remaining for this dessert.*

\* Please note the fruit at the side and the garnish in the photograph was included for illustration purposes only.

# Derry Clarke

## The Reluctant Chef

After twenty-one years running one of the best restaurants in Ireland, Derry Clarke is still at the top of his game. For someone who never wanted to be a chef, Derry has come a long way from his summer job as a pot washer. "I never set out to be a chef – far from it, really – but it all began for me in a restaurant in Kinsale called Man Friday's in the 1970s. I took a summer job as a pot washer and one day I found myself in the kitchen cooking... and here I am today."

After working in restaurants in Dublin and France, Derry opened L'Ecrivain in Lower Baggot Street, Dublin, and the rest, as they say, is history. "We are now in business over twenty years and I think a bit of a celebration is in order."

Derry has always had a very clear vision as to his food ethos. "I think that my style is all about cooking with the seasons. I source as much fresh Irish produce as I can. It's about supporting good local producers and keeping the food honest and real."

At home, Derry is very seldom found in the kitchen. "I don't do a lot of cooking at home – I like simple food and am very easy to please. A bacon sandwich is probably one of my favourite choices when I just want something quick and easy. But, like every meal I prepare at the restaurant, it's all down to the quality of the ingredients. That's what makes a simple bacon sandwich a great bacon sandwich."

The idea of using the best ingredients is one that Derry wants to pass on to anyone using his recipes. "For people on restrictive diets, or indeed for anyone who wants to prepare good food, the first step is to shop right. Whatever ingredients you get, make sure they are the best in terms of freshness and quality. For example, olive oil: if you get good-quality oil, you will see the difference in the food that you make.

"The list of ingredients for this book did create a bit of a challenge for me. Cooking is all about adding flavours; these flavours are the building blocks of the finished dish, so if you have to take some of these blocks out, you need to fill the gap with something else. After a while, I found I could fill the gaps quite easily and am very proud of my recipes in this book."

One flavour Derry didn't have much trouble doing without was salt. "I've started cutting back on the amount of salt I use in all my recipes over the last few years. Now I try to let my food speak for itself. Chicken should taste like chicken; carrots should taste like carrots." Derry's food ethos shines through in these recipes: "Remember, keep it simple. Buy the best quality and freshest ingredients you can – after that, you can't go wrong."

*L'Ecrivain, 2 Upper Baggot Street, Dublin 2. Tel: 01 6611919; www.lecrivain.com*

# Baked Cod Fillet, Sweet Mustard French Beans and Tomato Salsa

**Serves 8**

**FOR THE COD FILLET**

4 x 150g (5oz) cod fillets, skinned
   and cut in half
50g (2oz) Cheddar cheese, made with
   pasteurised milk, finely grated
2 level tbsp fresh white breadcrumbs
A pinch (¼ level tsp) freshly ground black pepper
2 level tbsp fresh mixed herbs, chopped
   (such as basil, chives and flat-leaf parsley)
1 tsp olive oil, for brushing

**FOR THE FRENCH BEANS**

400g (14oz) French beans, trimmed
4 level tsp mayonnaise
1 level tsp wholegrain mustard
1 small garlic clove, finely chopped
1 tsp runny honey

**FOR THE TOMATO SALSA**

130g (4½oz) ripe tomatoes, seeded and chopped
½ a mild red chilli, 7g (¼oz), seeded and finely chopped
1 level tbsp fresh mixed herbs, chopped
   (such as basil, chives and flat-leaf parsley)
A pinch (¼ level tsp) freshly ground black pepper

To prepare the herb crust for the cod, combine the Cheddar cheese in a bowl with the breadcrumbs and herbs. Season with pepper, then chill for 30 minutes to allow the mixture to firm up.

Preheat the oven to 200°C/400°F/Gas 6. When the mixture has firmed up sufficiently, carefully roll it out in between two sheets of greaseproof paper and cut into squares large enough to cover the pieces of cod. Arrange a piece of the crust on each one, pressing it down gently so that it sticks.

Brush a baking sheet with olive oil and add the herb-crusted pieces of cod. Bake for 6–8 minutes until the cod is just cooked through and the crust has browned.

Meanwhile, cook the French beans in a pan of boiling water until just tender. Drain well and then place in a bowl. Quickly add the mayonnaise, mustard, honey and garlic.

To make the salsa, place the tomatoes in a bowl with the chilli and herbs. Season with pepper and mix until well combined.

To serve, place a piece of herb-crusted cod on each plate and arrange a mound of the sweet mustard French beans to the side. Spoon the tomato salsa around the cod.

 ***Per portion*** *this dish provides 1 portion of vegetables and 2 protein exchanges.*

*If you have a daily allowance of dairy products, please note that there is cheese in this recipe which needs to be taken from your allowance.*

*If this recipe is served with boiled rice it would be suitable as a low fat main meal.*

*Check your daily allowances to see if you have enough remaining for this dish.*

# Chargrilled Fillet of Beef and Ratatouille

**Serves 4**

**FOR THE FILLET OF BEEF**

4 x 150g (5oz) beef fillets, well trimmed

1 tbsp olive oil

1 level tsp fresh thyme, chopped

A pinch (¼ level tsp) freshly cracked
   black pepper

**FOR THE RATATOUILLE**

1 tbsp olive oil

1 small onion, diced

1 garlic clove, crushed

½ red pepper, seeded and diced

100g (3½oz) courgette, trimmed and diced

130g (4½oz) aubergine, trimmed and diced

150g (5oz) canned chopped tomatoes, strained

½ level tbsp fresh oregano, chopped

A pinch (¼ level tsp) freshly ground black pepper

To prepare the steaks, mix the oil and thyme and use to coat the beef fillets; season with the fresh cracked pepper.

To cook the ratatouille, heat the olive oil in a large non-stick frying pan. Add the onion and garlic and sweat for 2 minutes until softened but not browned. Add the red pepper and sauté for another 2 minutes. Add the courgette and aubergine and cook for another minute, stirring to combine. Tip in the strained chopped tomatoes with the oregano. Stir well and season with pepper, then simmer for 5 minutes or until the vegetables are cooked through and tender, stirring occasionally. Keep warm.

To cook the steaks, preheat the oven to 190°C/375°F/Gas 5. Heat a cast-iron griddle pan (or frying pan) with a metal handle until very hot. Cook the steaks for 5–7 minutes and then transfer the seared steaks to the oven and cook for 10 minutes for well done, turning the steaks depending on their thickness.

To serve, divide the ratatouille among warmed plates and arrange the chargrilled beef fillets on top. Serve with couscous.

 *Per portion* this dish provides 2 portions of vegetables and 5 protein exchanges.

*Check your daily allowances to see if you have enough remaining for this dish.*

* Please note the garnish of a sprig of thyme in the photograph was included for illustration purposes only.

Derry Clarke

# Apple and Berry Strudel

**Serves 4**

1 large cooking apple
50g (2oz) caster sugar
A pinch (¼ level tsp) of ground cinnamon
25g (1oz) raspberries
25g (1oz) blackberries
25g (1oz) blueberries
40g (1½oz) butter
3 sheets filo pastry, thawed if frozen (45g (1½oz) each approximately)
2 level tbsp double cream, whipped

Preheat the oven to 160°C/325°F/Gas 3. Peel, core and roughly chop the apple. Place in a bowl with the sugar and cinnamon. Stir in the berries and set aside until needed.

Melt the butter in a small pan or in the microwave. Cut the filo sheets into quarters and then lay four quarters on a clean work surface. Brush lightly with the melted butter and layer up the rest of the filo.

Divide the apple and berry mixture among the layered-up filo piles. Hold a little back to arrange on the plates for presentation. Carefully fold over the filo to enclose the filling completely and brush the tops with a little of the rest of the melted butter. Transfer to a large baking sheet lined with non-stick parchment paper and bake the strudels for 15–20 minutes until the pastry is cooked through and golden brown.

To serve, arrange the apple and berry strudels on plates with a little whipped cream to the side.

 **Per portion** *this dessert provides ½ a portion of fruit.*
*Check your daily allowances to see if you have enough remaining for this dessert.*

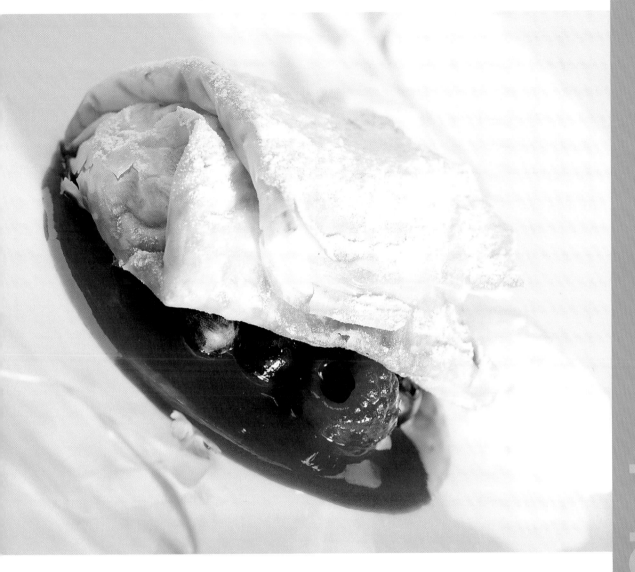

Domini Kemp

# Domini Kemp

*Itsa (Very Good) Bagel!*

When Domini Kemp moved to Ireland in 1983, good food was part of her life. "I used to work for my sister, all through my school years, when she had a small catering business. Then I finally decided in my twenties to go and get some sort of cooking qualification."

Heading for the bright lights of London, Domini enrolled at the world-famous Leiths Cookery School. "I did a year's training in Leiths in London, and from there I worked in a few London restaurants before moving back to Dublin and working in the Michelin-starred Peacock Alley for three years."

When Peacock Alley closed, Domini again turned to her sister, Peaches, and together they opened Itsabagel. "We started Itsabagel back in 1999 and have now developed it into a very successful food company with outside catering, restaurants and a wholesale and retail section as well."

Born in the Bahamas, Domini enjoyed something of a gourmet childhood. "We come from a family that loves good food and we were very lucky to be brought to good restaurants from a young age." For Domini, great food is a matter of simplicity. "I adore food that is properly seasoned and cooked with care and respect. It doesn't matter how simple or complex a dish is: careful seasoning and an understanding of cooking techniques are paramount for me."

Domini is also well known for her food writing and for her part in the RTÉ television show *Recipe for Success*, but at home she enjoys simple food with good ingredients. "I would say eggs are one of my very favourite ingredients, simply because they are so complete and versatile. We eat very casually at home, perhaps even very plain food. I am conscious of looking after our health, so mealtimes at home are light and nutritious. I spend a lot of time working on and refining fancier dishes, as well as testing recipes. So I find that I want to eat very simply at home and am conscious of trying to get at least five portions of fruit and vegetables into everyone each day."

For the recipes in this book, Domini found that the ingredients didn't pose too much of a conundrum. "If you were cooking in a restaurant, it would be challenging, but for home cooking it's relatively simple." She does, however, have some advice for people who will be trying her recipes. Apart from selecting the freshest ingredients available, Domini wants you to remember to have fun making – and above all tasting – this delicious food.

*www.itsabagel.com*

# Onion Tart with Fresh Herb Cream Cheese

**Serves 6**

### FOR THE PASTRY
170g (6oz) plain flour, plus extra for dusting
50g (2oz) ground rice flour
120g (4oz) butter
2 tsp cold water

### FOR THE FRESH HERB CREAM CHEESE
160g (5½oz) good quality cream cheese,
    made with pasteurised milk
2 level tbsp chopped fresh herbs such as
    parsley or basil
A pinch (¼ level tsp) freshly ground black pepper

### FOR THE ONION TOPPING
50g (2oz) butter, cut into rough cubes
650g (1lb 6oz) onions, finely sliced
3 garlic cloves, crushed
A pinch (¼ level tsp) freshly ground
    black pepper
1 level tsp sugar
1 level tsp fresh rosemary, sage or thyme,
    finely chopped

To make the pastry, mix all the ingredients together in the food processor. If the pastry doesn't fully come together to form one lump of dough, add a bit more water. Wrap in clingfilm and refrigerate until you are ready to roll it out.

To make the herb cream cheese, blend all the ingredients together with a fork, season with black pepper and chill until ready to use.

To make the onion mixture, place all the onion topping ingredients in a bowl and mix well to combine.

To make the tart, first preheat oven to 200°C/400°F/Gas 6. Roll out the pastry, on a lightly floured surface, to form one large circle (roughly 20cm/8in in diameter) or you can form 6 individual pastry rounds of about 10cm (4in) in diameter. Place the pastry base on a baking tray, top with the onion mixture and bake for 25–30 minutes or until the pastry is a nice golden brown.

Take out of the oven and serve sliced with a spoonful of the herb cream cheese on top.

*You can use white or red onions for this recipe. Make the pastry the night before, or even days before, and then freeze. Either way, do it first.*

**Per portion** *this dish contains 1½ portions of vegetables.*

*Check your daily allowances to see if you have enough remaining for this dish.*

* Please note the garnish in the photograph was included for illustration purposes only.

Domini Kemp

# Lasagne

**Serves 6**

FOR THE MEAT BASE

50ml (2fl oz) olive oil

1 kg (2¼lb) minced beef

A pinch (¼ level tsp) freshly ground
    black pepper

2 small onions, finely diced

2 x 400g (14oz) cans chopped tomatoes,
    strained well (strained weight = 480g)

300ml (½pt) water

4 garlic cloves, crushed

1 tbsp Worcestershire sauce

½ level tsp paprika

2 level tsp sugar

3 level tbsp fresh flat-leaf parsley, finely chopped

FOR THE BECHAMEL

60g (2½ oz) butter

60g (2½ oz) flour

400ml (14fl oz) milk

A pinch (¼ level tsp) freshly ground black pepper

120g (4oz) grated cheese (a mixture is best,
    such as Cheddar and mozzarella made with
    pasteurised milk)

6 x lasagne sheets (approx. 18g each)

Heat half the olive oil in a large frying pan until good and hot. Cook the mince over a high heat until well browned and season with pepper. This should take about 12–15 minutes. Have a colander ready, pour the mince into it and drain. Set aside and start making the tomato sauce.

Heat the remaining olive oil in a large saucepan and sweat the onions until soft. Add the tomatoes. Cook over a high heat to reduce the mixture. After about five minutes, add the remaining ingredients and the drained meat. Reduce the heat and cook for 20 minutes until the mince is fully cooked. Check the seasoning and adjust if necessary. Set aside and make the béchamel (white sauce).

To make the béchamel, melt the butter in a medium-sized saucepan, add the flour and stir vigorously. It will start to resemble polenta (this is called a *roux*). Cook over a gentle heat for two minutes – try not to let the saucepan burn. If the roux is starting to brown, remove from the heat and keep stirring. It is really important to cook the roux for this period of time, otherwise the béchamel will taste of uncooked flour. Add a good splash of milk and mix vigorously with a whisk. It will go all lumpy, but just keep whisking. Add more milk after each bit becomes incorporated and keep heating gently. When all the milk is added, cook for a further 5 minutes, stirring gently, ensuring the bottom of the pan is not burning. Season with pepper and add the grated cheese, stir and set aside. You are now ready to assemble the lasagne.

Put a layer of mince at the bottom of a medium-sized roasting tin or large casserole dish. Top with one layer of lasagne sheets, repeat and finish by pouring the béchamel directly on top. Preheat oven to 180°C/350°F/Gas 4 and cook for 45–60 minutes until the top is bubbling and lightly browned. Remove from the oven and allow to rest for 10 minutes before slicing and serving.

 **Per portion** *this dish provides 2 portions of vegetables, 4½ protein exchanges and 1 dairy exchange.*

*Check your daily allowances to see if you have enough remaining for this dish.*

# Pear and Apple Crumble

**Serves 8**

300g (11oz) plain flour
150g (5oz) butter, plus extra for greasing
150g (5oz) sugar
450g (1lb) cooking apples, peeled, cored and sliced
450g (1lb) pears, peeled, cored and sliced
125ml (4fl oz) single cream, whipped

Preheat oven to 180°C/350F/Gas 4. Grease a gratin (or pie) dish about 20 x 30cm (8 x 12in) with a little butter.

In a food processor, mix the flour, butter and 75g (2½oz) sugar. Process until the mixture resembles crumbs. Or you can do this by hand – mix the flour and sugar together and cut the butter into small pieces. Using your hands, rub the flour and butter lightly together to eventually create a crumb-like mixture. You can do this 24 hours in advance. Just chill and leave to rest overnight. In your greased dish, layer up the apples and pears with sprinkles of the remaining 75g (2½oz) sugar. Top with the crumble mixture and bake for about 35–40 minutes, or until the crumble topping is golden brown.

Serve on warmed plates with a tablespoon of lightly whipped cream per portion.

 **Per portion** *this dessert provides 1 portion of fruit.*

*Check your daily allowances to see if you have enough remaining for this dessert.*

Eugene McSweeney

## Eugene McSweeney

### Keep it Simple

After a career spanning forty years cooking in some of the world's best hotels and restaurants, Eugene McSweeney believes that, when it comes to good food, simplicity is best. "I remember watching my grandmother and my mother preparing the meals at home. Every meal they set before us was good, nourishing and tasty – and it was just that simple.

"My father would go out to the garden and dig up a few potatoes, bring them into the kitchen, wash them and then cook them in a big pot. After that, all they needed was some butter and it was a perfect meal. It was easy."

Originally from Portlaoise, Eugene has lived in Kilkenny for the past twenty-seven years. It was at Rockwell Catering College that Eugene started on his path as a trainee chef. "Nobody in my family had any training or connection with the catering world, so my career choice came as a bit of a surprise to all. And now, forty years later, I love cooking today as much as I did the day I started."

This love of cooking and food has taken Eugene around the world. His first job in

Ireland was at The Bailey pub on Duke Street, Dublin. "Then in 1978 I took the job of executive chef at Ireland's first five-star hotel, the Berkeley Court, in Ballsbridge. I spent four and a half years in the Berkeley Court and then decided to open my own place. So we bought Lacken House guesthouse in Kilkenny." Eugene and his wife spent the next eighteen years turning Lacken House into one of the best guesthouses in Ireland. "We won awards for the food, wine list and service at Lacken House, and I am very proud of what we achieved there."

Having had classical training when he began his life as a chef, Eugene always values any opportunity to get back to basics. "Today, I think people try too hard with food. We seem to want to mask the real flavour and taste. That's not to say sauces are bad, but sometimes all you need are good ingredients. I love fish and there is nothing better than fresh fish, simply cooked, with a sauce to enhance and not take away from the natural taste. This is what I call good cooking. So, keep it simple, buy the best you can and enjoy the real taste – that's what it's all about."

As for his favourite food, Eugene has no doubt what that is. "Duck – I am a sucker for duck. A duck breast pan-fried and than finished off in the oven: you can't beat it.

"When I saw the list of ingredients for this book, I thought it was going to be very difficult, but the more I played around with the different flavours, I found that it was actually very interesting. It made me think a lot about all the different combinations. You can still enjoy top-notch food even if you have to follow a certain diet, as long as the ingredients are good."

*Eugene McSweeney, Master Chef, BSc, Bleach Road, Kilkenny. Tel: 087 2530034;*
*Eugene.mcsweeney@gmail.com or eugenemcsweeney@webnode.com*

# Warm Lamb Salad with Yoghurt and Fresh Mint Dressing

**Serves 4**

200g (7oz) loin of lamb, trimmed
   and cut into small strips
250ml (9floz) water
1 small onion, cut in 2.5cm (1in) wedges
1 small carrot, scrubbed and cut into
   2.5cm (1in) pieces
1 small celery stick, trimmed and
   cut into 2.5cm (1in) pieces
1 bay leaf
3 parsley stalks
4 whole peppercorns

### FOR THE YOGHURT AND MINT DRESSING

1½ level tbsp low-fat mayonnaise
125g (4½oz) low-fat natural yoghurt
2 tsp fresh lemon juice
½ tsp honey
4 fresh mint leaves

### FOR THE SALAD

100g (3½oz) mixed salad leaves, freshly washed
   (may include butterhead, boston, bibb, webb,
   cos, romaine, iceberg, red leaf and rocket.
   Avoid spinach leaves.)
3 tbsp extra-virgin olive oil
2 tsp balsamic vinegar
A pinch (¼ level tsp) freshly ground black pepper

To prepare the lamb, place the water in a large pot and add the lamb with the onion, carrot, bay leaf, celery, parsley and peppercorns. Simmer for 20 minutes or until the lamb is tender. Remove from heat and allow to cool slightly. Drain off the cooking liquid, then remove the bay leaf, parsley stalks and peppercorns.

To prepare the yoghurt and mint dressing, put all the ingredients in a small bowl and whisk to combine. Add to the warm lamb and vegetable mixture.

To make the salad, combine the oil, vinegar and pepper in a bowl. Add the salad leaves and toss well to coat them in the dressing.

Serve the warm lamb and vegetables on warm plates with a little salad on the side.

 ***Per portion*** *this dish provides 1 portion of vegetables and 1½ protein exchanges.*

*If you have a daily allowance of dairy products, please note that there is yoghurt in this recipe, which needs to be taken from your allowance.*

*Check your daily allowances to see if you have enough remaining for this dish.*

Eugene McSweeney

75

# Beef with Leeks, Crème Fraîche and Rice

**Serves 4**

**FOR THE RICE**
220g (8oz) white rice
400ml (14fl oz) water
1 level tbsp fresh flat-leaf parsley, chopped
1 level tbsp fresh chives, chopped
1 level tsp freshly grated lemon zest

**FOR THE BEEF**
1 tbsp rapeseed or sunflower oil
100g (3½oz) leeks, sliced
1 small onion, thinly sliced
400g (14oz) striploin beef, cut in small strips
3 level tsp wholegrain mustard
200g (7oz) crème fraîche
A pinch (¼ level tsp) of paprika

To make the rice, bring the water to the boil in a medium-sized pan; once the water is boiling, add the rice. Stir once, reduce the heat and let it simmer for 15 minutes. Once cooked, strain off any excess water and then gently stir in the fresh herbs and lemon zest and combine well. Set the rice aside.

While the rice is cooking, prepare the beef strips in sour cream. Heat 1 tbsp of the oil in a pan and fry the onions and leeks, until they are softened but not coloured. Remove the onions and leeks from the pan and set aside. Then add another tbsp of oil to the pan and when it is very hot add the sliced beef and stir well, until it is well browned. Add the fried onion and leek back into the pan with the wholegrain mustard and crème fraîche. Simmer for a few minutes and then add the paprika. Let this simmer gently for 5 minutes to improve the flavour.

Serve in warmed bowls with rice.

 *Per portion* this dish provides 1 portion of vegetables and 3 protein exchanges. *Check your daily allowances to see if you have enough remaining for this dish.*

* Please note the garnish of fruit in the photograph was included for illustration purposes only.

# Quick and Easy Fresh Berry Ice Cream

**Serves 6**

200g (7oz) cream, lightly whipped
50g (2oz) caster sugar
200g (7oz) 60% reduced fat sour cream
1 tbsp fresh lemon juice
100g (3½oz) redcurrants
100g (3½oz) strawberries, sliced (fresh or thawed from frozen)

Place the cream into a medium-sized bowl, and whip until it forms soft peaks. Fold in the sugar. Gently fold in the sour cream until all ingredients are well blended.

You can use an ice cream maker if you have one at this stage or cover the bowl well and place in the freezer.

After one hour, remove and stir the ice cream to break down the ice crystals. Then replace the mixture back in the freezer. Repeat this process three times. Before you return the mixture to the freezer for the final hour, gently stir the fresh fruit (this prevents the fruit from becoming too hard). After 3 hours the ice cream will be hardened and ready to serve.

 ***Per portion*** *this dessert provides ½ a portion of fruit and ½ a dairy exchange.*

*Check your daily allowances to see if you have enough remaining for this dessert.*

# Georgina Campbell

## *Local, Seasonal, Simple*

It is no surprise to Georgina Campbell that she chose a career in food. "My father was a small farmer and my mother was a cookery teacher, so it was inevitable that I ended up working with food." However, after studying English and French in college, Georgina's plan was to work in the antiques business. "I was looking for work I could do from home, so I suggested to the *Irish Independent* that I would write a column about restoring old furniture and the like. The editor of what was then called the 'women's pages' met me for lunch and said what they were really looking for was a cookery columnist – and the next thing I knew, I was writing about food."

From that lunch meeting, Georgina went on to become one of Ireland's best-known food writers, with her guide series, *Georgina Campbell's Ireland*, now in its eleventh edition. "In the early eighties, there was nobody willing to get involved with a guide to eating out in Ireland; there were only the Egon Ronay guides. When they closed down in 1997, I decided to set up my own company and bring out my own guide."

Having spent so many years travelling around the country, Georgina has seen attitudes to food in Ireland transform over the years. "There has been an enormous change in attitudes. I think we have been through a very fussy stage over the last few years, but now I think we are beginning to get back to letting the food speak for itself. Today, my food philosophy is 'keep it simple'. Keep it local, keep it simple, keep it seasonal."

This is a philosophy that Georgina maintains at home. "I love vegetables and I grow my own; I love meat and fish, but I have to have fruit and vegetables. Having said that, you can't beat a good free-range egg. For me, working with food and eating in some of the best restaurants around the country, I like nothing better then to come home and prepare a simple meal – a really good omelette perhaps. Unfussy but excellent."

Regarding the recipes for this book, the key to success goes beyond the kitchen, according to Georgina. "Your shopping is the most important thing. Get your list organised and prioritise quality over quantity. The foundation of good health is built on the best-quality ingredients. I'm not a one hundred per cent organic enthusiast. I appreciate the value of organic food but it's not always possible to get good organic ingredients. I think it is far better to look for local, seasonal food – organic if possible – but always local.

"The important thing is to read the recipe from start to finish. You may never need to use it again but, for the first time, read the recipe. Above all, have fun with your cooking and enjoy your food."

*Georgina Campbell's recipes in this book are inspired by recipes from her seafood cookery book* From Tide to Table, *published in association with Bord Iascaigh Mhara (BIM), the Irish Sea Fisheries Board. For more information, visit www.ireland-guide.com*

# Fried Squid with Lime and Chilli Dressing

**Serves 4**

300g (10½oz) prepared squid pouches (allow to thaw completely if frozen)
½ level tsp (1.5g) Chinese five-spice powder (available in all good delis, Asian shops and supermarkets)
A pinch (¼ level tsp) freshly ground black pepper
2 tsp sunflower oil
4 tbsp sweet chilli sauce (available in all good delis, Asian shops and supermarkets)
Juice of 2 limes
20g (¾oz) fresh coriander leaves, roughly chopped

Cut along one side of each squid pouch and open it out flat. Score the inner side into a diamond pattern with the tip of a small, sharp knife, then cut the squid into triangles that are approximately 4cm (1½ in). Separate the tentacles, if large. Leave to drain on kitchen paper to remove any excess liquid.

Tip the squid into a large zip-lock bag and add the Chinese five spice and pepper, then shake well to coat the squid evenly.

Heat the oil in a wok or large frying pan until piping hot and smoking. Add the thinly sliced spiced squid and stir-fry for 30–40 seconds until cooked thoroughly through.

Remove the wok from the heat. Drizzle over the sweet chilli sauce, and lime juice and scatter most of the coriander on top. Quickly toss together until the squid is nicely glazed.

Arrange the squid on warmed plates and drizzle over any remaining dressing from the pan. Sprinkle with the remaining coriander and serve immediately.

*This is a wonderful Asian-inspired dish that is very quick to prepare. It is important to cook the squid thoroughly for food safety, however be careful not to cook it for too long as it can become tough and chewy.*

***Per portion*** *this dish provides ½ a portion of fruit and 2 protein exchanges.*

*Check your daily allowances to see if you have enough remaining for this dish.*

# Dover Sole with Lemon and Parsley Butter, Olive Mash and Roast Baby Leeks

**Serves 4**

### FOR THE OLIVE MASH

700g (1½lb) medium-sized potatoes (Kerrs Pink
   or Maris Piper are both good for mashing)
4 tbsp best-quality extra-virgin olive oil
120ml (4fl oz) milk

### FOR THE BABY ROASTED LEEKS

100g (3½oz) baby leeks, trimmed
2 tbsp olive oil
A pinch (¼ level tsp) of freshly ground black pepper
A squeeze of fresh lemon juice

### FOR THE FISH

50g (2oz) plain flour
4 x 150g (5oz) Dover sole fillets, skinned
   and bones removed
1 tbsp olive oil
50g (2oz) butter
Juice of 1 lemon
1 level tbsp fresh flat-leaf parsley, chopped
A pinch (¼ level tsp) freshly ground
   black pepper

To make the mash, peel and dice potatoes into 1cm (½in) cubes. Bring to the boil in 10 times their volume of water. Cook until potatoes are soft (see p. 282). While the potatoes are cooking, gently warm the milk in a small pan and set aside. You can prepare the leeks while the potatoes are cooking.

Preheat the oven to 180°C/350°F/Gas 4. Wash and remove the outer leaves from the baby leeks. Place in a large shallow roasting tin. Drizzle over the olive oil and toss to coat, then season with the black pepper and a squeeze of lemon juice. Place the leeks in the oven and roast for about 20 minutes until they have softened and lightly browned, stirring once or twice to ensure even cooking.

When the potatoes are cooked, drain and return to the warm pan. As you mash the potatoes, add in the warm milk in stages to make the mash nice and creamy. Finally add in the olive oil, mix well and then season with black pepper. Cover the pot of mash with a layer of tinfoil and then a tight-fitting lid to keep warm while you prepare the fish.

To prepare the fish, place the flour on a flat plate and season with a pinch of pepper. Use to dust the Dover sole fillets. Heat a large heavy-based frying pan. Add the oil and a knob of the butter and then fry the fillets for 2–3 minutes on each side until just tender. Transfer the fish to warmed plates and keep warm.

Add the remaining butter to the pan with the lemon juice. Cook for a couple of minutes, stirring constantly until the butter turns a very light brown. Stir in the parsley and season to taste.

To serve, spoon the lemon butter over the Dover sole fillets and serve at once with the baby roasted leeks and olive mash.

**Per portion** *this dish provides ½ a portion of vegetables, 2 potatoes and 4 protein exchanges.*

*If you have a daily allowance of dairy products, please note that there is milk in this recipe which needs to be taken from your allowance.*

*Check your daily allowances to see if you have enough remaining for this dish.*

# Double-Crust Apple Pie

**Serves 6**

**FOR THE SWEET SHORTCRUST PASTRY**
225g (8oz) plain flour, plus extra for dusting
A pinch (¼ level tsp) salt
120g (4½oz) butter
25g (1oz) caster sugar
3 tbsp cold milk
A little milk, for glazing
Icing sugar, for dusting

**FOR THE PIE FILLING**
700g (1½lb) cooking apples
75g (3oz) caster sugar
A little butter or 1 tbsp water

To make the pastry, sift the flour and salt into a mixing bowl. Chop the butter into small pieces and add to the sifted flour, then rub into the flour with the fingertips, holding well above the bowl to let air into the mixture as it falls back into the bowl. Continue until thoroughly blended and the mixture looks like fine breadcrumbs, then add the sugar and mix well. Sprinkle the milk over the mixture, and make the dough by cutting through the ingredients with a table knife or fork until everything clings together, leaving the bowl clean. Turn on to a lightly floured work surface and knead once or twice to make a smooth ball without cracks. Allow the dough to rest for 15–20 minutes before rolling out. (You can, of course, also use a blender or food processor to make the pastry.)

Preheat the oven to 200°C/400°F/Gas 6.

Now, on to the pie – on a floured work surface, roll out a third of the pastry to make a circle, and then line a 22.5cm (9in) pie plate with it. Peel, core and slice the apples, then spread half of them evenly across the pie plate. Sprinkle with the caster sugar and dot over a few small pieces of butter, or sprinkle with a tablespoon of water. Add the remaining apples, arranging them in a neat layer.

Roll out the remaining pastry to make a circle about 2.5cm (1in) bigger than the pie plate, and brush the rim with water to dampen. Cover the pie with the pastry lid and press the rim to seal the two layers of pastry together, then trim the edges and make several small slits with a sharp knife to let the steam escape. Pinch the edges together with your fingers or a teaspoon, to seal well and make an attractive finish, then brush the pastry lightly with milk and bake in the preheated oven for about half an hour, or until the pastry is

* Please note the garnish of fruit in the photograph was included for illustration purposes only.

nicely browned and crisp and the fruit is cooked. (Keep an eye on it towards the end of the cooking time, and reduce the oven temperature or cover the top lightly with crumpled tinfoil if it is browning too quickly.)

This apple pie is delicious served warm or cold, cut into slices on plates.

 **Per portion** *this dessert provides 1 portion of fruit.*

*Check your daily allowances to see if you have enough remaining for this dessert.*

# Kevin Dundon

## *Polishing the Dance Floor*

When Kevin Dundon was growing up, at home food was always a central point of debate. "There was always a deeply rooted passion for food in our house. My mother was a great cook and I spent many days just watching her prepare the meals. That's where the food bug took hold for me I suppose." When these culinary seeds began to bloom, Kevin left school and got a job in the Hollybrook Hotel in Clontarf, although his first job there was as far removed from the kitchen as you could get. "My first job was polishing the dance floor! From there I was promoted to kitchen porter. This was my first taste, so to speak, of a professional kitchen. But that small taste was enough to convince me that this was what I wanted to do – so I headed off to catering college." After culinary college Kevin won a scholarship and worked in Switzerland. "After Switzerland I spent seven years in Canada and finally returned to Ireland in 1994, to Dublin's Shelbourne Hotel."

Executive Chef at the Shelboune Hotel was a long way from polishing dance floors but Kevin's career was about to take another leap that would establish him as one of the best chefs in the country.

"We opened Dunbrody House twelve years ago. And I'd like to say that my wife Catherine and I wouldn't be where we are today without the great team that we have behind us. In the kitchen at Dunbrody to use only Irish ingredients where possible, we source all our ingredients locally and grow much of our own vegetables here in the gardens." Kevin has a simple philosophy when it comes to describing his style of cooking. "My cooking philosophy here in the restaurant or at home is really the same. If you get the best possible ingredients and do as little as possible to them then you can't really go wrong. Keep it simple and let the ingredients speak for themselves." When it comes to food, seasonality is very important to Kevin. "Eating in accordance with the seasons is hugely important to me; it was how I was brought up. If you buy local, seasonal food you will find that, apart from anything else, it works out cheaper in the long run and the food will be much fresher as well." Kevin is also well known to many from his books and his appearances on RTÉ's *The Afternoon Show* and on the culinary series *Guerrilla Gourmet*. "Working with food, it is very important to know where and how your food is produced," says Kevin. "This is hugely important for people cooking at home for family and friends. We must know that our food is safe, so it's important to be able to trust the source. Buying food directly from the producer at a farmers' market or from your local butcher or greengrocer is so much better than buying something that has been processed and packaged and then shipped halfway around the world. So do buy Irish whenever you can."

*Dunbrody Country House Hotel, Arthurstown, Co. Wexford. Tel: 051 389600;*
*www.dunbrodyhouse.com*

# Poached Salmon Pancakes with Chive Cream Cheese

**Serves 4**

**FOR THE PANCAKES**
50g (2oz) plain flour
1 small egg
150ml (¼pt) milk
Sunflower oil, for frying

**FOR THE SALMON FILLING**
225g (8oz) fresh salmon fillets, skinned and boned
225g (8oz) cream cheese, made with pasteurised milk
1 level tbsp fresh chives, snipped
Juice of 1 lemon

**TO SERVE**
25g (1oz) baby salad leaves, washed (may include butterhead, boston, bibb, webb, cos, romaine, iceberg, red leaf and/or rocket. Avoid spinach leaves.)
2 level tbsp wholegrain mustard dressing (see p. 95)
A pinch (¼ level tsp) freshly ground black pepper
4 lemon wedges, to serve

To make the pancakes, sift the flour into a bowl, then make a well in the centre. Break the egg into the well and add a little of the milk. Mix the liquid ingredients together, then gradually beat in the flour until smooth. Beat in enough of the remaining milk until you have achieved the consistency of thin cream. Cover with clingfilm and leave to stand in the fridge for 20 minutes.

Heat a heavy-based frying pan. When hot, brush with the minimum of oil. Pour in a small amount of the batter, about a quarter of the mix is right. Swirl it around until it is evenly and thinly spread over the bottom. Cook over a moderate to high heat for about 1 minute or until the edges are curling and the underside is golden. Flip over and cook the second side for 30 seconds or so until golden.

Turn the pancake on to a plate and repeat until you have four pancakes in total, lightly oiling the pan between pancakes. Leave to cool, then using a 5cm (2in) cutter that is 5cm (2in) deep stamp out three circles from each pancake to make small pancakes (5cm each in diameter).

The simplest way to poach your salmon fillets is to double wrap each one in clingfilm, nice and secure. Place wrapped fillets in a large bowl and cover with boiling water. Let them sit

* Please note the garnish in the photograph was included for illustration purposes only.

and poach in the water for 7–10 mins or so until they are an opaque, very pale pink colour. Remove fillets from the water. Unwrap and break the poached fillets up into flakes. Set aside.

Whip the cream cheese in a bowl with the chives and lemon juice.

To serve, line the cutter with clingfilm and set on a serving plate. Put a pancake round in the bottom of the cutter and add a spoonful of the chive cream cheese. Cover with a layer of the poached salmon and then add another spoonful of the chive cream cheese. Repeat these layers and finish with a pancake round. Carefully remove the cutter and repeat until you have four in total.

Place the salad leaves in a bowl, season and add enough of the dressing to lightly coat the leaves. Add a small pile to each plate. Drizzle around the remaining dressing and garnish with the lemon wedges.

*Food trends come and go but this is one recipe that has stood the test of time at Dunbrody and once you've taken your first bite you'll understand why. It is perfect for a dinner party, as it can be prepared several hours in advance, ready to be brought back to room temperature and dressed with a little salad.*

**Per portion** *this dish provides ½ a portion of vegetables, 2 protein exchanges and ½ a dairy exchange.*

*As there is some milk and a large amount of cream cheese (which contains some milk) in the recipe, we have counted them together as ½ a dairy exchange (see allowances above).*

*Check your daily allowances to see if you have enough remaining for this dish.*

# Seared Fillet of Beef with Crispy Onions and Horseradish Dressing

**Serves 4**

### FOR THE BEEF

450g (1lb) fillet of beef (please ask your
butcher for well-hung beef)
1 tbsp olive oil

### FOR THE HORSERADISH DRESSING

2 level tbsp mayonnaise
1 level tbsp creamed horseradish, available
in all good supermarkets and delis
Juice of ½ lemon

### FOR THE CRISPY ONIONS

Sunflower oil, for deep-frying
50g (2oz) plain flour
½ large onion, thinly sliced

### TO SERVE

50g (2oz) mixed salad leaves, washed
(choose from butterhead, boston, bibb,
webb, cos, romaine, iceberg, red leaf and
rocket. Avoid spinach leaves.)
1–2 tbsp balsamic vinaigrette (see p. 95)

Preheat oven to 200°/400°F/Gas 6. Heat an ovenproof griddle pan until very hot.
Add the olive oil to the pan and then add the beef and brown on all sides for about 30
seconds on each side until you have achieved a nice, well-browned crust. Then place the
beef in a roasting tin and roast in the hot oven for about 30 minutes. Remove from the heat
and cut into the centre of the fillet to make sure it is cooked to well done. If not, return it to
the hot oven for a further 5 minutes to make sure it is cooked through with no pink meat
visible. Once cooked, leave the beef to rest in a warm place until the beef has relaxed.
This will take at least 10 minutes.

To make the horseradish cream, place the mayonnaise in a small bowl with the creamed
horseradish and lemon juice. Mix until well combined. Cover with clingfilm and chill in the
fridge until needed.

To make the crispy onion rings, heat the oil in a deep-fat fryer to 180°C (350°F) if you have
one. Or heat about 7.5cm (3in) of sunflower oil in a wok or deep-sided pot. To test when
the oil is hot enough, drop a small piece of white bread into the oil; it should immediately
float to the top and turn golden brown in about 30 seconds.

Place the flour on a plate and then dip each onion slice in the flour until they are lightly
dusted, shaking off any excess flour. Deep-fry the onion rings for 4–5 minutes or until
golden brown. Spread them out on kitchen paper and allow to cool and crisp up.

While they are cooling lift them occasionally so that they do not all stick together.

To serve, when the beef has rested, transfer it to a carving board. Use a very sharp carving knife to cut it into slices. Place the mixed salad leaves in a bowl and add enough of the vinaigrette to lightly coat the leaves.

Arrange the beef on plates with a dollop of the horseradish cream, a little dressed salad and a small pile of the crispy onion rings.

You can accompany this dish with some freshly cooked rice.

 **Per portion** *this dish provides 1 portion of vegetables and 3½ protein exchanges.*

*Check your daily allowances to see if you have enough remaining for this dish.*

# Wholegrain Mustard Dressing

1 level tsp wholegrain mustard
2 tsp honey
Juice of ½ a lemon
A pinch (¼ level tsp) caster sugar
A pinch (¼ level tsp) freshly ground black pepper
170ml (6fl oz) olive oil
2 tsp hot water, optional
A pinch (¼ level tsp) fresh thyme, chopped finely

To make the dressing, mix the mustard, honey, lemon juice, sugar and pepper together in a bowl. Whisk in the olive oil and, if the dressing seems too thick, correct the consistency with hot water. Whisk in the chopped thyme and allow the dressing to rest until required.

This dressing will keep for 2 weeks.

# Balsamic Vinaigrette

100ml (3½fl oz) balsamic vinegar
100ml (3½fl oz) olive oil
A pinch (¼ level tsp) fresh thyme, chopped finely
Juice of ½ lemon

Whisk all the ingredients together and store in an airtight jar.

This dressing will keep for 2 weeks.

*The analysis for a portion of these dressings has been included in the coding on p. 94.*

**Kevin Dundon**

# Bread and Butter Pudding

**Serves 6**

75g (3oz) butter, at room temperature
12 slices medium-sliced white bread
150g (5oz) blueberries

**FOR THE CUSTARD**
300ml (½pt) cream
300ml (½pt) milk
4 egg yolks
75g (3oz) caster sugar, plus extra to dust

Generously butter an ovenproof dish. Remove the crusts from the bread and, using the remaining butter, butter both sides of each slice and then cut each slice into quarters.

Arrange a single layer of the bread triangles, slightly overlapping in the bottom of the buttered dish. Scatter over some of the blueberries, then place another layer of the bread triangles on top and scatter over the remaining berries. Press down gently with a fish slice or spatula.

To make the custard, heat the cream and milk in a pan until it almost comes to the boil. Remove from the heat. Meanwhile, whisk together the egg yolks and sugar in a large heat-proof bowl set over a pan of simmering water until thickened and the whisk leaves a trail in the mixture. Remove from the heat and beat into the cream mixture until well combined.

Pour two-thirds of the custard over the layered-up bread triangles and leave to stand for about 30 minutes or until the bread has soaked up all of the custard.

Preheat the oven to 180°C/350°F/Gas 4. Pour the remaining custard over the soaked bread-and-butter triangles and arrange the rest of the bread triangles on top. Press down firmly with a fish slice so that the custard comes halfway up the bread triangles. Bake for 30–35 minutes until the custard is just set and the top is golden brown.

To serve, bring the bread and butter pudding straight to the table and have separate jugs of the custard to hand around so that everyone can help themselves.

 **Per portion** *this dessert provides ½ a portion of fruit and ½ a protein exchange.*

*While you don't usually think of desserts as having a lot of protein this recipe contains approximately ½ an egg per portion and therefore it has been counted in the protein allowances for this recipe.*

*If you have a daily allowance of dairy products, please note that there is milk in this recipe, which needs to be taken from your allowance.*

*Check your daily allowances to see if you have enough remaining for this dessert.*

# Leylie Hayes

*Food Should Be Fun*

A chance trip to East Cork set our chef off on her career in cooking. Leylie Hayes decided to do a short cookery course at the world-famous Ballymaloe Cookery School and has never looked back. "I was twenty-one; I had done a few different jobs but nothing that I wanted to call a career. Then one day I saw that Ballymaloe was offering some short two-week courses and I decided to give it a go. I just fell in love with the whole ethos and style of Ballymaloe cooking. After that short course, I went back and spent a year at the school – and here I am today."

After working in Dublin and London, Leylie returned to open Avoca's first restaurant. "Would you believe that was seventeen years ago? I was the first and only chef in Kilmacanogue, and today Avoca has over a hundred chefs in nine different locations around the country."

Leylie's love of food comes from her family background and home life. "When I was growing up in Dublin, my family was very food-orientated. My mother was a very good cook and, as a family, we always took time to eat together. I found that when I went to

Ballymaloe, the passion and ethos for good food was something I remembered from my own family, and I think that's why it had such an effect on me. I took one of my daughters down to Ballymaloe a couple of years ago and, even at thirteen, she was completely blown away by the place."

Now, as the executive head chef at Avoca, Leylie has taken her food ethos one step further. "At Avoca we pride ourselves on the quality of the ingredients that we use, from only using free-range eggs and real butter to the best olive oil. For us, it's all about using the best ingredients available. I base my food ethos at Avoca on what I learned at Ballymaloe: if you start with really good ingredients, then you can't go far wrong."

Of course, Leylie has her own favourites when it comes to good food. "I don't have a sweet tooth. I prefer savoury foods – I like nothing better than a really good bowl of soup. I also love to experiment with spices and herbs, and then sometimes I just need comfort food like a really good homemade shepherd's pie.

"I did find the challenge to create recipes for this book very interesting – I found that because I use a lot of fresh herbs and spices, I was able to come up with recipes that are really tasty and nutritious. Remember, the key to cooking is good ingredients. One mistake that people make is that they don't read the recipe from start to finish. I firmly believe that anyone can cook: read the recipe, set all the ingredients out, and then start cooking. Have fun, make your food an event and – above all – enjoy yourself."

*Avoca Handweavers, Kilmacanogue, Bray, Co. Wicklow.*
*Tel: 01 2867477; www.avoca.ie*

* Please note the garnish of mint in the photograph was included for illustration purposes only.

# Courgette and Mint Soup

**Serves 4**

100g (3½oz) potato, peeled and cut into thin slices
50g (2oz) butter
60g (2oz) onion, chopped
A pinch (¼ level tsp) freshly ground black pepper
600ml (1pt) chicken stock (use 1 suitable stock cube to 600ml water)
250g (9oz) courgettes, finely sliced
2 level tbsp fresh mint, chopped
4 tbsp cream

To double-boil the potato, bring potato to the boil in four times its volume of water. Once boiled, throw the water away, and replace with the same volume of fresh boiling water. Boil until potato is soft through and then strain and set aside. (see p. 282)

Place a generous saucepan on a low heat and melt the butter. Add the chopped onion and sauté on a low heat until softened. Add the double-cooked potato and season with the black pepper. Add the chicken stock and bring to the boil; simmer gently for 5 minutes until the onion is cooked through.

Add the courgette and bring back to the boil, then reduce the heat and simmer for 5 minutes. Remove from the heat, add mint and cream and liquidise until smooth.

Serve in warmed bowls.

 ***Per portion*** *this dish provides 2 portions of vegetables and ½ potato.*

*If you are on a fluid restriction remember to count this soup as part of your daily intake.*

*Do not use homemade chicken stock. Ask your dietitian to suggest a suitable stock cube.*

*Check your daily allowances to see if you have enough remaining for this dish.*

# Summer Lemon and Pork Burger with Roasted Red Peppers and Rocket

**Serves 4**

450g (1lb) minced leg of pork (you can ask your butcher to do this for you)
1 small onion, very finely diced or minced
2 level tsp fresh thyme and sage, finely chopped
Zest of 1 lemon
A pinch (¼ level tsp) of freshly ground black pepper
1 egg
320g (11oz) red peppers, cut into 4 halves and seeds removed
2 tsp olive oil
4 wholemeal baps, cut in half
50g (2oz) fresh rocket leaves
20g (¾oz) crème fraîche, to serve

Preheat oven to 180°C/350°F/Gas 4. Place pork, onion, herbs, lemon zest, egg and black pepper in a bowl and mix well. Shape into 4 round burgers and set aside. Be careful not to make your burgers too thick as they may dry out during cooking.

Rub the pepper halves with olive oil and roast in the preheated oven for 25–30 minutes until softened. Remove the roasted peppers from the oven and place them in a zip-lock bag (or similar), seal the bag and leave them to cool. Once cooled, you may peel the peppers if you like; they will be easy to peel as the skin will have lifted from the pepper.

To cook the burgers you can cook them on a hot, non-stick pan for 15–20 minutes until the meat is cooked well done. Or you can roast them in the oven for about 20 minutes. Slice into the centre of one of the burgers to check that they are well done.

Toast the baps, place a burger on each bottom half and top with a half-roasted pepper, followed by some fresh rocket and a teaspoon of crème fraîche on each to serve.
Place the bap tops to the side of each burger.

 *Per portion* this dish provides 1½ portions of vegetables and 3½ protein exchanges.
*Check your daily allowances to see if you have enough remaining for this dish.*

Leylie Hayes

# Lemon Tart

**Serves 6**

### FOR THE SHORTCRUST PASTRY
100g (4oz) plain flour
75g (3oz) butter, diced
15g (½oz) caster sugar
1 egg yolk

### FOR THE LEMON TART FILLING
200g (8oz) caster sugar
Juice of 5 lemons
Grated zest of 3 lemons
4 eggs
175ml (6fl oz) double cream, whipped
2 level tsp icing sugar, for dusting

To prepare the shortcrust pastry, preheat oven to 180°C/350°F/Gas 4. Sift the flour into a bowl and rub in the butter until the mixture resembles fine breadcrumbs. Stir in the caster sugar, then add the egg yolks and mix to form a dough; add a little cold water if necessary. Wrap in clingfilm and leave to rest in the fridge for 20–30 minutes. (Or it can be left in the fridge overnight.)

Roll out the dough on a lightly floured work surface and use to line a deep 18cm (7in) loose-bottomed flan tin. To bake blind, cover the pastry with greaseproof paper and fill with baking beans (either ceramic ones or any raw dried beans, which you can reuse for baking blind). Bake in the pre-heated oven at 180°C/350°F/Gas 4 for 20 minutes. Remove the beans and greaseproof paper and return the pastry case to the oven for 5–10 minutes, until very lightly coloured. (After removing the beans and paper, you could brush the partly cooked pastry with lightly beaten egg white before returning it to the oven. This helps to form a seal and keeps the pastry crisp when you add the filling.)

To prepare the lemon tart filling, put the sugar and lemon juice in a large bowl and stir until the sugar has dissolved. Add the lemon zest, whisk in the eggs and finally stir in the cream. For best results leave the filling, well covered, in the fridge overnight. (If you don't leave it overnight it will separate during cooking, giving a custard bottom and foamy top.)

The next day, preheat oven to 140°C/275°F/Gas 1. Remove mixture from fridge and stir gently to combine it again. Pour the filling into the baked pastry case and cook it for 1 hour, until set. Remove from the oven and leave to cool.

To serve, dust the tart with icing sugar and then caramelise it, if you like, under a very hot grill.

 *__Per portion__ this dessert provides ½ a portion of fruit and 1 protein exchange.*

*While you don't usually think of desserts as having a lot of protein, this recipe has approximately 1 egg per portion and therefore it has been counted in the protein allowances for this recipe.*

*Check your daily allowances to see if you have enough remaining for this dessert.*

Leylie Hayes

# Liz Moore

## The Belle of Belle Isle

A wise man once said that "a passion for food can not be denied for long" and this proved true enough for Liz Moore. "From the very beginning I came from a foodie family. Most chefs I know say that their passion for food all began at their mother's sides in the kitchen and it was the same for me. However, I never intended to cook for a living. I wanted to do many other things but I think cooking chose me." Liz, who is originally from Co. Monaghan, now runs the superb Belle Isle Cookery School in Co. Fermanagh. "I had been living in Italy for a number of years and when I came home in 1997 I started cooking to earn some money, because I could and as a sort of stop-gap really. I started doing private parties and events like that." After a while Liz found that she had started her own catering company. "I said I would continue to do this until I found a proper job. My base was in Co. Meath and I was travelling the country, but I started to work more and more in Northern Ireland. I ended up working for the Duke of Abercorn who had the idea of opening a cookery school and so Belle Isle was created." Set on an island, The Belle Isle Cookery School offers a varied range of residential and non-residential cookery courses and is the only cookery school of its type in the region. "The estate was bought over twenty years ago and was set up initially as holiday accommodation and the cookery school grew from this concept." Over the years Liz has concentrated on creating food that is full of taste using the ingredients that are available on the estate or from producers in the region. "I like simplicity. I love when other chefs do swirls and foams and so on but I like my food to look like food. I am very into colour and herbs. It's simple with robust flavours – that's what my cooking is all about. For me it is also essential to eat seasonally. The reason for eating with the seasons, apart from the fact that it is good for your pocket, is that seasonal eating is much better for your body as well." With this in mind what foods are top of the list for Liz? "I like all foods really but I do like something a bit different when I am out. At home I like nothing better than a poached egg on toast. Again it's all about good ingredients; once you have that you can't really go wrong."

Was it a challenge for Liz to create recipes for this cookbook? "The challenge opened my eyes. We are used to working with people who have allergies to nuts or wheat or dairy products, but I found that with the recipes in this book it's all about treating the ingredients in a different way and, of course, using the freshest products. Have fun cooking, shop well to get the best ingredients you can and read the recipe from start to finish. After that, *enjoy*."

*Belle Isle School of Cookery, Lisbellaw, Enniskillen, Co. Fermanagh, Northern Ireland, BT94 5HG. Tel: +44 (0)28 6638 7231; fax: +44 (0)28 6638 7261; www.irish-cookery-school.com*

# Courgette Fritters with Horseradish and Yoghurt Dip

**Serves 4**

**FOR THE HORSERADISH AND YOGHURT DIP**
175ml (6fl oz) double cream
1 tbsp (approx. 20g) mayonnaise
4 tbsp (approx. 120g) plain yoghurt
75g (3oz) fresh horseradish,
    peeled and very finely grated

**FOR THE COURGETTE FRITTERS**
200g (7oz) courgettes
1 shallot, finely chopped
200g (7oz) cottage cheese,
    made with pasteurised milk
50g (2oz) plain flour
1 level tbsp fresh basil, finely chopped
2 free-range eggs
A pinch (¼ level tsp) freshly ground pepper
2 tbsp olive oil

First make the horseradish cream. Whip the cream until it stiffens. Fold in the mayonnaise, yoghurt and grated horseradish to taste. Be warned, fresh horseradish is strong, so err on the side of caution! Set aside in an airtight jar in the fridge. It will keep happily for 2–3 days.

To make the fritters, wash the courgettes and trim the ends. Grate the courgettes over a tea towel and then squeeze out as much water as you can. Then mix all of the fritter ingredients together in a bowl.

Heat the oil in a heavy-based frying pan and fry spoonfuls of the mixture, flattening slightly on both sides, for 2 minutes or so until golden. The size of the fritters is up to you. They work well as canapés when they are made small or you can serve them instead of potatoes when they are bigger. Allow an extra minute or two cooking time on either side if they are bigger.

Once the fritters are cooked, set aside on some kitchen paper to drain off any excess oil. Arrange on plates and serve with a dollop of horseradish cream.

***Per portion*** *this dish provides 2 portions of vegetables, ½ a protein exchange and 1 dairy exchange.*

*Check your daily allowances to see if you have enough remaining for this dish.*

Liz Moore

# Braised Chicken with Root Vegetables

**Serves 6**

50g (2oz) butter
1 tbsp olive oil
1 large free-range chicken (approx. 2kg/4½lb)
½ level tsp freshly ground black pepper
900ml (1½pts) water
2 level tbsp fresh tarragon, chopped
4 garlic cloves, peeled but left whole
2 bay leaves
800g (1¾lb) potatoes, peeled and cut into 1cm (½in) cubes
210g (7½oz) carrots, peeled and cut into batons
210g (7½oz) leeks, well washed and sliced
360g (12½oz) onions, roughly chopped into quarters
15g (½oz) fresh parsley, chopped

Preheat oven to 180°C/350°F/Gas 4. Melt the butter with the olive oil in a large casserole pot. Season the chicken with pepper and add the chicken to the pan, skin side down, and turn to brown all over. Add the water and the tarragon, garlic and bay leaves. Bring to the boil and then place in the oven for 40 minutes.

Cut the potatoes into 1cm (½in) cubes. Bring to the boil in 10 times their volume of water. Boil the potatoes until soft. Remove from heat and strain. (See p. 282)

Remove the casserole from the oven and add carrots, leeks and onion quarters. Replace in the oven for a further 25 minutes. Remove from the oven and add the cooked potatoes.

To serve, carve the chicken and serve 125g in warmed, deep bowls with the vegetables and plenty of the hot broth. Garnish with chopped parsley.

**Per portion** *this dish provides 1½ portions of vegetables, 1½ potatoes and 5 protein exchanges.*

*If you are on a potassium restriction, discard the broth.*

*Check your daily allowances to see if you have enough remaining for this dish.*

* Please note the garnish of a sprig of fresh parsley in the photograph was included for illustration purposes only.

* Please note the garnish of fruit in the photograph was included for illustration purposes only.

# Orange Cake with Raspberry Oil

**Serves 12**

**FOR THE CAKE BATTER**
250g (9oz) unsalted butter, softened
250g (9oz) caster sugar
4 free-range eggs, separated
2 tbsp milk
Zest of 1 orange
250g (9oz) plain flour

**FOR THE RASPBERRY OIL**
150g (5oz) fresh raspberries
150ml (5fl oz) olive oil
50g (2oz) icing sugar

**FOR THE ICING**
125g (4½oz) icing sugar
5 tsp fresh lemon juice

Preheat the oven to 180°C/350°F/Gas 4. Grease and line a 22cm (9in) loose-bottomed cake tin.

To make the raspberry oil, start by pounding the soft raspberries to a pulp in a large bowl. Whisk in the oil and icing sugar until well combined. Leave to sit for 5–20 minutes to allow the flavours to develop. Pass through a sieve to remove the seeds.

Cream together the butter and sugar very well until smooth and creamy. Beat in the egg yolks one at a time with the milk. Beat in the orange zest and flour.

Whisk the egg whites to form peaks and fold gently into the cake mixture. Spoon the mixture into the tin and bake for about 45–50 minutes or until the cake feels firm to the touch and a skewer, once inserted, comes out clean. Allow the cake to cool in its tin, then carefully remove and transfer to a plate.

Stir the icing sugar and lemon juice together. Pour the icing over the top of the cooled cake.

Cut into slices and arrange on plates, served with the raspberry oil.

 *Per portion* this dessert provides ½ portion of fruit.

*Check your daily allowances to see if you have enough remaining for this dessert.*

# Neven Maguire

## *Enjoy What You Eat*

Neven Maguire always knew that he wanted to be a chef. "I was the only boy in my school to do home economics. I don't know what started it all off, but my mother was a major influence on me where cooking was concerned."

After training with Paul Rankin and then in a number of five-star hotels in Germany, Luxembourg and Spain, Neven returned to his hometown of Blacklion, Co. Cavan, to take over the running of the family restaurant, MacNean House and Restaurant. "I like to be hands-on with everything here in Blacklion. We run an intimate operation with just ten guest rooms. I enjoy the personal touch and I love to meet each and every customer when they come to eat and stay here. I like to let my diners know who my suppliers are and I feel this adds to the experience of eating locally produced food. I think we all need to support our local butchers and farmers; food that has been produced in your area will always taste better than something that has travelled across the globe before it gets to your plate."

Neven has become one of Ireland's best-known and best-loved chefs through his many cookery books and TV shows. "Over the years, I have seen the growth of a huge foodie movement here in Ireland. We now have wonderful food festivals and events all over the country. More and more people are interested in where their food comes from, and the growth in the number of farmers' markets is great to see. With this increased interest in good food, we are seeing better food being produced. We have wonderful bakers, cheesemakers and other artisan food producers around the country and I hope that we will continue to support them all."

At home, Neven loves cooking for his family and friends. "I love pasta and it's great to have nothing more than a plate of pasta with a good sauce. However, I have to say that my all-time favourite meal has to be grilled rib-eye steak with some chunky, home-made chips. Again, it's all about the ingredients: rib-eye is one of the less expensive cuts of steak but I think it has more flavour than sirloin or fillet."

We asked Neven to create a special Christmas menu for this book. "Christmas comes only once a year, so do make an effort to get the best ingredients you can. A free-range turkey is a good start, and try to support your local producers if you can. I always believe that good cooking starts with good shopping, and the time you spend gathering your ingredients is just as important as the effort you put in in the kitchen. I hope you enjoy my Christmas menu and I hope you will have a wonderful time cooking and eating my recipes!"

*MacNean House and Restaurant, Blacklion, Co. Cavan.*
*Tel: 071 9853022; www.macneanrestaurant.com*

# Warm Salad with Pear and White Cheddar Cheese

**Serves 4**

### FOR THE SALAD

1 tbsp rapeseed oil, for frying croutons

1 slice of thick white bread, cut into crouton cubes

60g (2oz) mixed organic leaves, freshly washed
(such as butterhead, boston, bibb, webb,
cos, romaine, iceberg, red leaf and rocket.
Avoid spinach leaves.)

2 medium ripe pears, peeled, cored and sliced

Juice of ¼ of a lemon

60g (2oz) cherry tomatoes, quartered

60g (2oz) mature white Cheddar, made with pasteurised milk

### FOR THE DRESSING

2 tbsp balsamic vinegar

4 tbsp olive oil

1 tsp golden syrup

1 level tsp wholegrain mustard

A pinch of brown sugar

First make the salad dressing by putting the vinegar, oil, golden syrup, mustard and sugar into a container with a lid. Shake vigorously until thick and smooth and keep in the fridge.

Heat the oil in a frying pan and fry the bread cubes until golden brown and crunchy. Keep warm until ready.

Prepare four individual portions of the salad leaves on plates or in small bowls. Add the pear slices and sprinkle with lemon juice. Crumble the cheese on top and sprinkle over the croutons and cherry tomatoes. Drizzle the dressing around to serve.

 **Per portion** *this dish provides 1 portion of fruit, ½ a portion of vegetables and ½ a dairy exchange.*

*Check your daily allowances to see if you have enough remaining for this dish.*

# Roast Crown of Turkey, Sage and Onion Stuffing, Seasonal Vegetables and Crispy Potatoes

**Serves 8**

**FOR THE STUFFING**

75g (3oz) butter

1 small onion, diced

1 level tsp fresh sage, chopped

175g (6oz) fresh white breadcrumbs

A pinch (¼ level tsp) freshly ground black pepper

**FOR THE TURKEY**

4.5kg (10lb) ready-prepared turkey crown

75g (3oz) butter, at room temperature

1 garlic clove, crushed

Finely grated zest of 1 orange

1 level tbsp fresh flat-leaf parsley, chopped

1 level tsp fresh thyme, chopped

**FOR THE GRAVY**

1 level tbsp plain flour

300ml (½pt) chicken stock (use ½ a suitable chicken stock cube to 300ml water)

A pinch (¼ level tsp) freshly ground black pepper

**TO SERVE**

Pan-fried Brussels sprouts with nutmeg (see p. 120)

Roast carrots with garlic and parsley (see p. 120)

Crispy roast potatoes with rosemary and red onion (see p. 121)

Preheat the oven to 190°C/375°F/gas 5. To make the stuffing, heat a frying pan and melt the butter. Add the onion and sage and cook for a few minutes, until softened but not coloured. Stir in the breadcrumbs, mixing well to combine. Season with freshly ground black pepper. Wrap the stuffing in buttered tinfoil and mould into a large sausage shape. This can be cooked in the oven for 25–30 minutes.

Next, prepare the turkey crown. Cream the butter in a bowl until very soft and then add the crushed garlic, orange rind, parsley and thyme. Beat well, until thoroughly blended. Gently loosen the neck flap away from the breast and pack the flavoured butter right under the skin – this is best done using gloves on your hands. Rub well into the flesh of the turkey, then re-cover the skin and secure with a small skewer.

Place the turkey crown in the oven and calculate your time. You should allow 20 minutes per 450g (1lb) plus 20 minutes, so a joint this size should take 3 hours and 40 minutes.

Cover loosely with foil and remove this about 40 minutes before the end of the cooking time. The turkey crown will cook much quicker than a whole turkey, so make sure to keep basting. To check if the turkey is cooked, pierce a fine skewer into the chest part of the crown – the juice should run clear. When cooked, cover with foil to rest and keep warm. To make the gravy, skim all the fat from the cooking juices in the pan and then pour off all but 3 tablespoons of the juices from the roasting tin. Stir the flour into the pan residue and cook, stirring over a low heat, until golden. Gradually add the stock with any remaining juices, stirring all the time. Bring to the boil and let bubble for 2–3 minutes, until thickened. Season with freshly ground black pepper.

To serve, carve the turkey crown into slices and arrange 125g on warmed plates with the cooked stuffing, Brussels sprouts with nutmeg, roasted carrots with garlic and parsley and crispy potatoes. Pour the gravy into a warmed gravy jug and hand around separately.

*See p. 121 for information on what this entire Christmas dinner provides.*

# Pan-Fried Brussels Sprouts with Nutmeg

**Serves 8**

320g (11oz) Brussels sprouts, trimmed and halved

2 tbsp olive oil

40g (1½oz) butter

½ level tsp freshly grated nutmeg

A pinch (¼ level tsp) freshly ground black pepper

2 small red onions, peeled and sliced

1 level tsp fresh flat-leaf parsley, chopped

Bring a large pan of water to the boil and add in the sprouts. Cook for 5–10 minutes until just tender and drain them. Keep warm.

Heat the oil and 25g (1oz) of the butter in a large frying pan until foaming. Toss in the red onions and fry over a medium heat for 5–8 minutes, until softened and golden. Add the blanched Brussels sprouts and the nutmeg and fry for a further 3–5 minutes until golden and softened. Season well with pepper, add parsley and serve with the rest of the butter melting on top.

# Roast Carrots with Garlic and Parsley

**Serves 8**

375g (13oz) carrots, scrubbed

2 tbsp olive oil

2 level tsp caster sugar

1 garlic bulb, broken into individual cloves, unpeeled

1 tsp balsamic vinegar

2 level tbsp fresh flat-leaf parsley, chopped

Preheat the oven to 190°C/375°F/Gas 5. Cut the carrots into 1cm (½in) slices on the diagonal and place in a roasting tin. Drizzle with the olive oil and sprinkle lightly with the sugar. Toss well to coat and roast for 15 minutes.

Remove the carrots from the oven and scatter over the unpeeled garlic, tossing until evenly combined. Roast for another 15 minutes, until the carrots and garlic are tender and lightly golden.

To serve, drizzle over the balsamic vinegar and scatter over the chopped parsley, again tossing until evenly coated then, tip into warmed bowls to serve at the table.

# Crispy Potatoes with Rosemary and Red Onion

**Serves 8**

1.3kg (3lb) potatoes
100g (3½oz) plain flour
1 level tsp fresh rosemary, finely chopped
A pinch (¼ level tsp) freshly ground black pepper
1 small red onion, finely sliced
2 tbsp olive oil

Peel and cut the potatoes into 1cm (½in) cubes and bring to the boil in 10 times their volume of water, then cook until tender. Dry thoroughly (see p. 282).

Preheat oven to 200°C/400°F/Gas 6. Spread the flour out on a large flat dish, sprinkle with the rosemary and pepper and then gently roll the potato cubes in the seasoned flour until all pieces are lightly coated.

Add the floured potato cubes to a baking tin, drizzle the olive oil over them and bake in the oven for 30 minutes or until golden brown and crispy. Ten minutes before the potatoes are finished, add in the chopped onion to bake with the potato.

*Per portion* this Christmas dinner provides 2 portions of vegetables, 1½ potatoes and 6 protein exchanges.

*Do not use a homemade chicken stock. Ask your dietitians to suggest a suitable stock cube.*

*Check your daily allowances to see if you have enough remaining for this dinner.*

# Passion Fruit Tart

**Serves 10**

100g (3½oz) butter, diced
175g (6oz) plain flour, sifted,
    plus extra for dusting
⅛ level tsp salt
50g (2oz) caster sugar
1 egg yolk
½ tbsp double cream
Egg wash (1 full-size egg with
    1 tbsp milk) for brushing
25g (1oz) icing sugar, to brulée (optional)

**FOR THE RASPBERRY SAUCE**

100g (3½oz) raspberries, plus 4 (16g) small
    raspberries to decorate each portion
1 level tsp icing sugar

**FOR THE FILLING**

5 small eggs
175g (6oz) caster sugar
Finely grated zest and juice of 2 lemons
6 passion fruits, halved and pulp scooped out
225ml (8fl oz) double cream

To make the pastry, place the butter, flour, salt and sugar in a food processor and blend for about 10 seconds until the mixture resembles fine breadcrumbs. Add the egg yolk and cream and mix again briefly. Do not over-work or the pastry will become tough. Bring the pastry together into a ball and wrap in clingfilm, then place in the fridge for at least 3–4 hours to firm up.

To make the raspberry sauce, blend the raspberries and icing sugar in a food processor for 1 minute. Pass through a sieve into a bowl, cover with clingfilm and keep chilled until ready to serve.

Preheat the oven to 180°C/350°F/Gas 4. When the pastry is chilled, roll out on a lightly floured work surface and use to line a 20cm (8in) diameter flan ring. Cover with foil, then fill with baking beans and bake "blind" for about 20 minutes until the pastry is golden brown. Remove from the oven; discard the baking beans and the foil and brush the warm pastry case with the egg wash.

Reduce the oven temperature to 160°C/325°F/Gas 3.

To make the filling, combine the eggs in a large bowl with the sugar, lemon rind and passion fruit pulp and juice, then stir in the lemon juice and cream. Blitz with a hand blender, then pass through a sieve into a jug. This extracts as much flavour from the passion fruit as possible.

Pour the mixture into the pre-baked pastry case. Bake for 30–40 minutes until set and slightly wobbly in the centre. Turn off the heat and leave the tart to cool completely in the oven.

The tart can be served as it is, or you can brown the top by coating with icing sugar and putting briefly under a very hot preheated grill.

To serve, place a slice of tart on each plate, dot some raspberry sauce to the side and decorate with raspberries.

 **Per portion** *this dessert provides ½ a portion of fruit and ½ a protein exchange.*

*While you don't usually think of desserts as having a lot of protein, this recipe has ½ an egg per portion and therefore it has been counted in the protein allowances for this recipe.*

*Check your daily allowances to see if you have enough remaining for this dessert.*

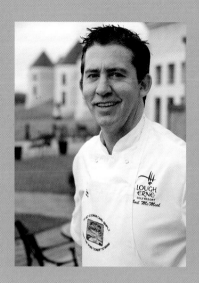

# Noel McMeel

## *Never Forget the Field You Were Foaled In*

Whether he's making potato farls in his family's kitchen or cooking for the Queen, President Clinton or President Bush, Noel McMeel always remembers where he has come from. "My roots are still firmly set in the soil of my family farm and the values I learned there as a child. The lessons I learned then, about the quality and integrity of good food, are probably more relevant to me now than ever before."

Indeed, this innate sense of quality was what led Noel to create a vegetarian banquet for Paul McCartney's wedding while he was head chef at Castle Leslie. "My father always said, 'Never forget the field you were foaled in', which simply means to never forget where you come from. And I haven't. Absolute simplicity and respect for the ingredients is paramount. I believe in letting the flavours sing for themselves. My dishes may appear complex but, in fact, they tend to be cooked quite simply – with rigorous attention to the freshness and seasonality of the ingredients."

After training at the Northern Ireland Hotel and Catering College in Portrush, Noel began his career in the kitchen with celebrity chef duo Jeanne and Paul Rankin, at their restaurant in Belfast. "In 1988, I got a scholarship to the USA and got to work in some very prestigious kitchens. I have been very lucky over the years with the places I have worked and the people I have met."

Some of these prestigious people and places include the Watergate Hotel in Washington DC, with Jean-Louis Palladin, and a stint at Chez Panisse in San Francisco, working with his culinary heroine, chef-patron Alice Waters. Back home in Ireland, Noel is in demand with RTE and the BBC, and he regularly travels the world as a demonstrator, judge and guest chef for special occasion dinners. "My roots are firmly back here now, heading up the kitchen at the Lough Erne Golf Resort."

Noel describes his style of food as fresh and uncomplicated. "I like to think that I have a very simple goal: finding, preparing and serving fresh food in season and sharing this knowledge with others. There will always be fads in the food world but, for me, the words of the moment are – organic, fresh, taste, simple, changing seasons, local, real cooking, knowledge – and they will be the lasting food trends. I have always been convinced that the best-tasting food is organically grown and harvested in ways that are ecologically sound, by people who are taking care of the land for future generations. After all, food like that speaks for itself."

Noel was delighted to share some of his recipes for this cookbook. "Cooking and eating good food is a very important part of life. It's great to see more and more people getting involved and getting back into the kitchen. But cooking and food should be about more than merely fuelling the body. Cooking is more than just the act of putting food on a plate; we should all make it an important part of our lives."

*Lough Erne Golf Resort and Hotel, Enniskillen, Co. Fermanagh.*
*Tel: 048 66323230; www.lougherngolfresort.com*

# Ravioli of Goat's Cheese with Fresh Basil and Sweet Plum Tomato Sauce

**Serves 4**

**FOR THE PASTA DOUGH**

225g (8oz) plain or pasta flour,
plus extra for dusting

2 free-range eggs

2 free-range egg yolks

1 tbsp olive oil

A pinch (¼ level tsp) of salt

**FOR THE FILLING**

150g (5½oz) soft goat's cheese made with pasteurised milk, crumbled

A pinch (¼ level tsp) freshly ground black pepper

1 free-range egg, beaten

**FOR THE SAUCE**

100g (3½oz) unsalted butter

½ shallot (approx. 15g), finely chopped

10 basil leaves (approx. 5g), chopped

½ garlic clove, chopped

1 level tbsp fresh parsley, chopped

400g (14oz) ripe plum tomatoes, skinned, seeded and finely chopped

To prepare the pasta dough, place the flour, whole eggs, yolks, oil and salt in a large bowl and, using your hands, knead to form a firm dough. Cover with clingfilm and place in the fridge for at least 5 hours.

Meanwhile, make the filling. Place the crumbled goat's cheese in a bowl, season it with freshly ground black pepper and leave to one side. Next make the ravioli. When the dough has rested, put the dough through a pasta machine or roll it out on a well-floured, cool surface until you have two large flat rectangular shapes, approximately 60cm (24in) long. Keep dusting all the time with flour so the dough doesn't stick to your surface or your rolling pin.

Place 1 tablespoon of the goat's cheese filling on the dough roughly 4cm (1½in) apart. Glaze in between each spoon of filling with the beaten egg mixture, then place the second pasta sheet on top. Press along the edges of each spoon of filling with your fingers. Using a pastry wheel (or a very sharp knife) cut into 10cm (4in) squares to create your ravioli.

To cook, simply bring a pot of water to boiling point (100°C), then add in the ravioli for 8 minutes. Remove with a slotted spoon and keep warm.

For the sauce, heat the butter in a frying pan and, when it starts to froth and turn golden brown, add the shallot, basil, garlic, parsley and tomatoes. Cook for a minute or two.

Serve the ravioli in warmed wide-rimmed bowls and pour over the plum tomato sauce.

 ***Per portion*** *this dish provides 2 portions of vegetables, 1 protein exchange and 1 dairy exchange.*

*Goat's cheese is a soft cheese. To ensure food safety it should be made with pasteurised milk and cooked thoroughly i.e. make sure it is steaming hot all the way through.*

*Check your daily allowances to see if you have enough remaining for this dish.*

# Roast Free-Range Chicken with Crispy Fried Potatoes and Carrot and Parsnip Mash

**Serves 6**

1 whole free-range chicken
2 tbsp olive oil
1 level tbsp black peppercorns

Zest of 1 orange and the remaining orange quartered
1 level tbsp fresh thyme, finely chopped
3 bay leaves

**FOR THE POTATOES**

800g (1¾lb) potato, cubed
1 small onion, quartered
60ml (2½fl oz) rapeseed oil
½ level tsp fresh rosemary, finely chopped
2 garlic cloves, minced

**FOR THE CARROT AND PARSNIP MASH**

260g (9oz) parsnips, peeled and cut into chunks
400g (14oz) carrots, peeled and cut into chunks
50g (2oz) unsalted butter
A pinch (¼ level tsp) freshly ground black pepper

Preheat the oven to 190°C/375°F/Gas 5. Weigh the chicken.

Rub the olive oil into the skin of the chicken. Roughly crush the peppercorns and mix with the orange zest and thyme and rub this into the skin. Cut the orange into 4 and put it inside the body cavity of the chicken along with the bay leaves.

To roast the chicken, allow 20 minutes cooking time for every 450g (1lb) of meat. Place the chicken in a large roasting tin and cover the bird loosely with a large piece of tinfoil. Every 30 minutes or so, baste the bird by taking it out and using a large spoon to pour the cooking juices over the top of the bird.

While the chicken is roasting, prepare the potatoes. Peel and dice them into 1cm (½in) cubes. Bring to the boil in 10 times their volume of water (see p. 282). Once the potatoes are soft through, strain and leave them to cool. In a bowl, combine the cooked potato cubes, onion, oil, rosemary and garlic and toss to coat. Transfer to a foil-lined baking pan.

Meanwhile prepare the carrot and parsnip mash. Boil the parsnips and carrots in boiling water for about 15 minutes until tender. Then drain. Using a potato masher, mash the vegetables together with the butter and season with freshly ground black pepper. Set aside to keep warm.

When the chicken is cooked, the juices will run clear when you spear it with a skewer. Remove the bird from the oven, cover with tinfoil and allow to rest.

While the chicken is resting increase the oven temperature to 220°C/425°F/Gas 7, and then place potato cubes and onion mixture in to roast for 20–30 minutes until crispy and golden brown.

To serve, carve the roast chicken (allowing only 125g/5oz chicken per portion) and serve on warmed plates with crispy roast potatoes and carrot and parsnip mash on the side.

 **Per portion** *this dish provides 2 portions of vegetables, 1½ potatoes and 5 protein exchanges.*

*Check your daily allowances to see if you have enough remaining for this dish.*

# Blueberry Cheesecake

**Serves 14**

100g (3½oz) butter
250g (9oz) digestive biscuits, crushed
600g (1¼lb) pasteurised cream cheese
100g (3½oz) icing sugar
300ml (10fl oz) double cream, whipped
200g (7oz) fresh blueberries
To serve: 10 blueberries per portion

1 x 18cm (7in) round cake tin with removable base or 14 x 5cm (2in) small moulds

Melt the butter in a saucepan over a low heat. Add the crushed digestive biscuits to the melted butter and use a wooden spoon to mix well. Place the mixture into a lined 18cm (7in) tin with a removable base or fill the base of each of your small moulds. Flatten down the biscuit mixture with a spatula or the palm of your clean hand and then place the cake tin or small moulds in the fridge until cool.

Place the cream cheese in a bowl and use a wooden spoon to beat, add the icing sugar, then fold in the whipped cream. Add the fresh blueberries. Remove the cake tin or moulds with the cooled biscuit mixture from the fridge and pour over the cream cheese topping. Only fill the small moulds about ¾ full with the cream cheese topping. Cover very well with clingfilm and place in the fridge for at least two hours to chill and set.

Slice and serve with blueberries on the side.

 **Per portion** *this dessert provides ½ a portion of fruit.*

*Check your daily allowances to see if you have enough remaining for this dessert.*

Noel McMeel

# Oliver Dunne

## *Find Your Passion*

Luck can have a lot to do with the way your life turns out, and for Oliver Dunne it was by complete chance that he became one of the best chefs in Ireland. "I tried a few different things before I got into the kitchen. I went to college to study to be an engineer, then I studied business, and I even sold shoes on Henry Street in Dublin for a time. I had no interest in food or cooking and then, one day, I was offered a job in Gotham Restaurant. I took the job for the money, as I knew nothing about cooking. But I learned fast!"

After a few years working in some of the best-known restaurants in Dublin, Oliver headed for the bright lights of London. "It was my twenty-first birthday and, tragically, a friend of mine had just died in a house fire in Scotland. It was a turning point for me and I felt I needed to do something worthwhile with my life; I wanted to spend my time doing something I really enjoyed and not just move from job to job. I had worked in Peacock Alley and Roly's Bistro, and when I went to London I knew that cooking was what I wanted to do."

In London, Oliver worked with Gary Rhodes and Gordon Ramsay before heading home to Dublin's Clarence Hotel. "Over the years, I have found that the food I cook has changed. We cook seasonally here in the restaurant, so we only cook with what is fresh right now. This, I think, is how food should be enjoyed: each season has its highlights so, when you get fresh seasonal ingredients, you can't go far wrong."

At home, Oliver likes simple, no-fuss, tasty food. "I only eat at home once a week but, when I do cook, I like to keep it simple. I love big, hearty, comfort food like stews and roast chicken."

Oliver relaunched the restaurant Bon Appétit in 2006 and was awarded a Michelin star after only one year. He has channelled his trademark flair into this book. "When it came to creating these recipes, I wanted to make sure that all the ingredients would be easy to source and that the meals would be fun to make. My recipes use ingredients that are readily available all year round – but always just remember to enjoy your cooking."

*Bon Appétit, 9 James Terrace, Malahide, Co. Dublin.*
*Tel: 01 8450314; www.bonappetit.ie*

# Poached Hens Egg with Soft Polenta and Fresh Parmesan

**Serves 4**

4 eggs
250ml (9fl oz) water or chicken stock (if using chicken stock, make up with a ¼ of a
    suitable chicken stock cube to 250ml water)
50g (2oz) polenta flour
2 level tbsp freshly grated Parmesan made with pasteurised milk
1 level tsp fresh chives, finely chopped

To poach the eggs, bring a medium-sized pot of water to the boil. As the water is gently boiling, crack each egg off the side of the pot and gently let the egg fall into the water. Do this very carefully; do not drop the egg into the water. Let the eggs poach in the water for 6 minutes until the whites and yolks are completely opaque and firm. Then remove each poached egg from the water with a slotted spoon and plunge into a bowl of iced water, to prevent them cooking any further.

In a medium-sized pot, bring the 250ml water (or chicken stock) to the boil, whisk in the polenta flour and let this simmer for 15 minutes, stirring constantly. The polenta should now be thick and creamy.

Season the polenta with most of the grated Parmesan and chives.

Fill a pot or ceramic bowl with just-boiled water and place the poached eggs into the boiling water for 30 seconds to warm them up.

To serve, place the polenta in warmed bowls with a poached egg on top and garnish with the reserved grated Parmesan.

***Per portion*** *this dish provides 1 protein exchange.*

*If you have a daily allowance of dairy products, please note that there is cheese in this recipe, which needs to be taken from your allowance. Do not use a homemade chicken stock. Ask your dietitian to suggest a suitable stock cube.*

*Check your daily allowances to see if you have enough remaining for this dish.*

# Roasted Fillet of Pork, Citrus Couscous, Roast Pepper and Courgettes

**Serves 4**

**FOR THE PORK**
600g (1¼lb) pork fillet
1 tbsp olive oil, for frying

**FOR THE PEPPERS AND COURGETTE**
160g (5½oz) red peppers, sliced and seeded
160g (5½oz) yellow peppers, sliced and seeded
130g (4½oz) courgettes, sliced
2 tbsp olive oil
2 garlic cloves, finely chopped
½ tsp honey

**FOR THE COUSCOUS**
Zest and juice of 1 lime
Zest and juice of 1 lemon
Zest and juice of 1 orange
½ level tsp of ground cinnamon
1 tbsp olive oil
2 tbsp boiling water
400g (14oz) couscous
1 level tsp fresh coriander, chopped
1 level tsp fresh basil, chopped

Mix the zest and juice of the lemon, lime and orange with olive oil and boiling water. Add this mixture to the couscous in a large ceramic or glass (or any heatproof) bowl and mix well. Cover with clingfilm and place the bowl over a pot of boiling water to cook. The couscous will expand as it cooks. It will take about 10 minutes. Once it is cooked, add the cinnamon and stir in the chopped fresh herbs.

Preheat the oven to 180°C/350°F/Gas 4. To cook the pork, remove any excess fat and sinew. Place a large pan on a high heat, add the oil and then add the pork to the hot pan to brown for a minute on each side to seal in the flavours, turning the meat to brown it all over. Then place the fillet in a small roasting tin and have it ready to go into the oven.

To prepare the peppers, place them in a bowl with the courgettes, olive oil, garlic and honey and mix well. Then place the peppers in an ovenproof dish and put them in the oven at the same time as the pork. Roast both the peppers and the pork in the oven for about 30 minutes. Remove and allow to rest.

To assemble, slice the pork into thin rounds. Place some couscous on each plate, with slices of the pork on top and strips of roasted peppers and courgettes on the side to garnish.

 *Per portion* this dish provides ½ a portion of fruit, 2 portions of vegetables and 4½ protein exchanges.

*Check your daily allowances to see if you have enough remaining for this dish.*

Oliver Dunne

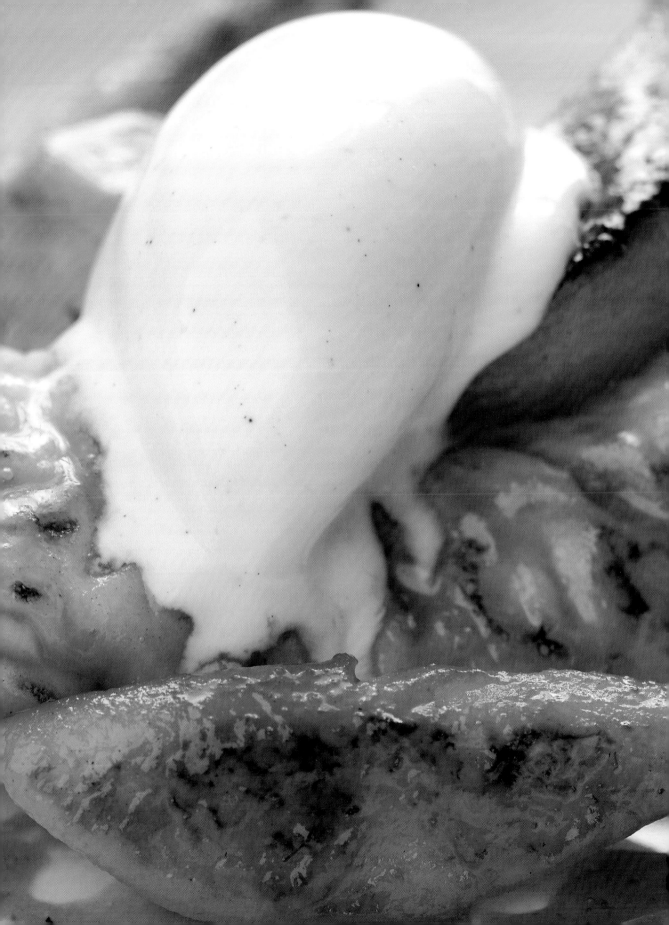

# Caramelised Pear Crêpe with Vanilla Ice Cream

**Serves 4**

**FOR THE CRÊPE BATTER**

50g (2oz) plain flour

1 egg

2 tsp olive oil

240g (8½oz) best-quality vanilla ice cream, to serve

4 level tbsp caster sugar

175ml (6fl oz) milk

**FOR THE CARAMELISED PEARS**

2 large pears

1 tbsp olive oil

2 tbsp honey

2 whole cloves

To make the crêpes, sift the flour into a large mixing bowl with a sieve held high above the bowl so the flour gets air into it. Add the sugar. Now make a well in the centre of the flour and sugar and break the egg into it. Then begin whisking the egg – any sort of whisk or even a fork will do - incorporating the flour from around the edge of the bowl as you do so. Next gradually add small quantities of the milk, still whisking (don't worry about any lumps as they will eventually disappear as you whisk). When all the milk has been added, add the olive oil and use a rubber spatula to scrape any elusive bits of flour from around the edge into the centre, then whisk once more until the batter is smooth, with the consistency of thin cream.

Next peel the pears, quarter them, then remove the core and cut each of the pear quarters in half. Heat a large frying pan, add the oil and then the fruit. Cook briefly to colour and then remove. Add the honey to the still hot pan and, when it starts to caramelise, add the fruit back in and the cloves. Coat the pears well in the caramel liquid. Set aside.

To cook the crêpes, get your frying pan very hot, then turn the heat down to medium and use a ladle to spoon about 2 tablespoons of crêpe liquid into the pan. As soon as the batter hits the hot pan, tip it around from side to side to get the base evenly coated with batter. It should take only half a minute or so to cook; you can lift the edge with a palette knife to see if it's tinged gold as it should be. Flip the pancake over with a pan slice or palette knife – the other side will need a few seconds only – then simply slide it out of the pan onto a plate.

Stack the pancakes as you make them between sheets of greaseproof paper on a plate set over a pan of simmering water, to keep them warm while you make the rest. You will need 4 in total. When completed, put some of the caramelised pear into each one and roll up. Serve 1 roll per person on a plate with a single scoop of vanilla ice cream on top.

 ***Per portion*** *this dish provides 1 fruit portion and ½ a dairy exchange.*

*Check your daily allowances to see if you have enough remaining for this dessert.*

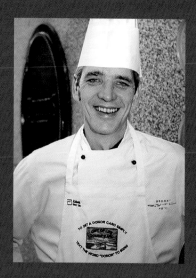

# Patrick McLarnon

## *Practice Makes Perfect*

It was at Portrush Catering College that Patrick McLarnon trained to become one of Ireland's award-winning chefs. But Patrick's interest in food started a long time before that, when he was at home in Portglenone, Co. Antrim. "My interest in food was instilled during my childhood at home. Mealtimes in our house were always a pleasure and I learned a lot from my mother. At thirteen years old, I knew I wanted to be a chef. When I left Portrush Catering College I got my first job in Kees Hotel in Donegal."

However, the bright lights of the city were calling Patrick and he was soon on his way to Fitzpatrick Castle Hotel in Killiney. "I learned a lot at both these hotels but I wanted to travel. I was given some contacts in Germany so I headed over there and then went on to work in Switzerland and France, where I learned a lot about the different styles and techniques of cooking."

Armed with all this culinary knowledge, Patrick returned to Ireland in the early 1990s and took the top job at Brooks Hotel in Dublin. "I have been here in Brooks now for over 11 years. The culinary ethos in the hotel is very good – Brooks is the only Dublin hotel in the *Bridgestone Guide* and we have a good team of homegrown talent in the kitchen."

Distilled from all his experience, Patrick's food philosophy is very simple. "Where I can, I source organic and local produce and then I like to meddle very little with the raw material. Once I have good local food that is well produced, I like to reflect this, without fuss, on the plate. For example, I want a breast of chicken to look like a breast of chicken, nothing else."

So, if he had to choose, what would Patrick's favourite food be? "I love lamb. I have an allotment and recently I headed out there, armed with a barbecue and some really nice lamb. The weather was great and I dug some lovely fresh onions and garlic out of the ground and cooked them with the lamb on the barbecue. There is nothing like the experience of growing and cooking your own food. You know you are getting good produce when you grow it yourself."

Patrick admits he found the list of ingredients for this book posed some difficulty when he began working on his recipes. "I had to sit and think about all the limitations before I could get started. I had to replace the pinch of salt with something else, so I had to look at other ways of injecting flavour into the dishes. But I think I managed to achieve some very tasty recipes for the book – I hope people enjoy making and eating my dishes. Remember, practice makes perfect but the main thing is to enjoy your cooking."

*Brooks Hotel, Drury Street, Dublin 2. Tel: 01 6704000; www.brookshotel.ie*

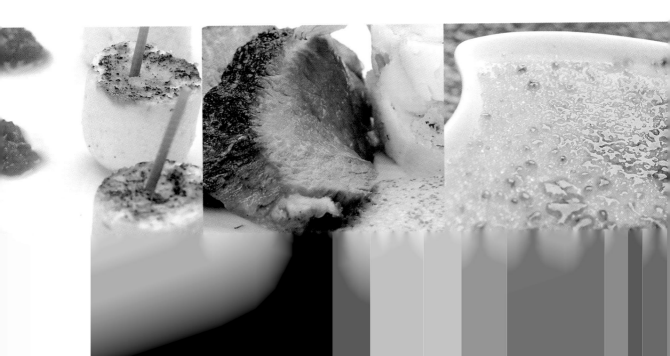

# Chicken Sausage with Red Pepper Jam

**Serves 4**

**FOR THE RED PEPPER JAM**

1 large red pepper, seeded and roughly chopped
Juice of half a lemon
2 tbsp honey

**FOR THE CHICKEN SAUSAGE**

150g (5oz) skinless chicken breast fillet, well chilled
1 egg, well chilled
A pinch (¼ level tsp) white pepper
A pinch (¼ level tsp) ground nutmeg
A pinch (¼ level tsp) fresh tarragon, finely chopped
100ml (3½fl oz) cream
1 level tbsp icing sugar, sieved on to a plate

To make the red pepper jam, purée the pepper in a food processor and then transfer to a small saucepan. Add the lemon juice and bring to the boil for 1½ minutes, then reduce the heat, add the honey and simmer for a further 3 minutes. Place in a small bowl or jar and leave to cool. This can be made in advance.

To make the chicken sausage ensure all the ingredients and work utensils are well chilled. Chop the chicken roughly, place in a food processor with the egg and liquidise until smooth. Transfer the mixture to a bowl and season with the white pepper, nutmeg and tarragon, then carefully pour in the cream, stirring all the time until mixed through. Place in the fridge to chill for at least 30 minutes but up to 24 hours.

To shape and cook the chicken sausage, place a medium-sized pan of water on the hob to boil. Spoon a quarter of the chicken sausage mix on to the centre of a 30cm (14in) sheet of clingfilm about 2cm (¾in) from the edge nearest you to form into a sausage shape approximately 10cm (4in) long, then gently roll away from you as evenly as you can. Keep the twist as tight as you can and then tie the ends with string or thread. Repeat the process until you have four sausages in total. Practice makes perfect!

Place your clingfilm-covered chicken sausages into the water, reduce the heat to a simmer and cook for approximately 5–7minutes depending on the thickness of each sausage. Remove from the heat and allow the sausages to chill slightly, then carefully remove the clingfilm.

\* Please note the garnish in the photograph was included for illustration purposes only.

Cut each sausage into 3 pieces and dip one end of each piece into the icing sugar.

Heat a large frying pan and place the sugared sausage pieces, 3 or 4 at a time, on to the pan, working quickly just to caramelise the sugar and make each end nice and crispy. Remove them and keep warm.

To serve, divide the sausages, crispy side up, on to plates and spoon a little of the red pepper jam on the side.

 ***Per portion*** *this dish provides ½ a portion of vegetables and 1½ protein exchanges.*

*Check your daily allowances to see if you have enough remaining for this dish.*

# Roast Rump of Lamb with Turmeric Potatoes, Cucumber and Mint Sauce

**Serves 4**

600g (1¼lb) rump of lamb, in 2 pieces

**FOR THE MARINADE**

125g (4½oz) Greek yoghurt
1 small onion, peeled and chopped
4–5 garlic cloves, peeled
25g (1oz) fresh mint, chopped
½ a lemon, chopped
1 level tsp cumin
12 black peppercorns

**FOR THE CUCUMBER AND MINT SAUCE**

½ cucumber, grated
125g (4½oz) Greek yoghurt
Juice of half a lemon
1 garlic clove, crushed
25g (1oz) fresh mint, chopped
A pinch (¼ level tsp) freshly ground
    black pepper

**FOR THE TURMERIC POTATOES**

800g (1¾lb) potatoes, peeled and diced into 1cm (½in) cubes
1 level tsp turmeric
15g (½oz) red chilli, seeded and chopped
1 garlic clove, chopped
⅛ level tsp white pepper
2 tbsp olive oil for frying

To prepare the marinade, liquidise all of the listed ingredients and set aside.

To marinate the lamb, first trim the lamb of any excess fat, then place the lamb in a generous-sized bowl or container and coat the meat well with the marinade. Leave the lamb to sit in the marinade for a day or two, well covered, in the fridge.

To prepare the lamb, preheat the oven to 200°C/400°F/Gas 6. Remove lamb from the marinade and pat the meat dry with a kitchen towel. Then brown the lamb in a hot pan with a little oil. Place in a roasting tin and roast in the hot oven for 10–15 minutes until the meat is cooked through to well done. Turn the meat over once or twice while it cooks. Remove the lamb from the oven and let it rest for 10–15 minutes in the roasting tin.

To prepare the turmeric potatoes, boil the cubed potatoes in 10 times their volume of water. Add 1 tsp of turmeric to the water. Once the potatoes are soft through, remove from the heat and strain. (The potatoes could be prepared to this point the day before.)

(See p. 282)

\* Please note the garnish in the photograph was included for illustration purposes only.

Add the oil to a hot pan and fry the chilli and garlic. Add the cooked potato cubes and fry until golden brown and crisp.

To prepare the cucumber and mint sauce, combine all of the ingredients listed above to create the sauce and refrigerate until you are ready to serve.

To serve, slice the lamb and divide neatly on to warm plates. To present the potatoes on the plate in an interesting manner, place a 10cm (4in) round pastry ring on the plate and press the potatoes gently into the ring. Remove the ring to leave a round of potato on the plate and pour a spoon of cucumber and mint sauce over.

 **Per portion** *this dish provides 1 portion of vegetables, 2 potatoes, 4 protein exchanges and ½ a dairy exchange.*

*Check your daily allowances to see if you have enough remaining for this dish.*

# Vanilla Crème Brûlée

**Serves 6**

1 vanilla pod
500ml (17fl oz) cream
9 egg yolks
75g (3oz) sugar
A sprinkle of Demerara brown sugar

6 x 150ml (5oz) ramekins or similar-sized pudding moulds

Preheat the oven to 130°C/250°F/Gas ½. Split the vanilla pod in half lengthwise and scrape the seeds out. Place the vanilla seeds in a pan with the cream and heat slowly to let the vanilla flavours release into the cream. Do not allow it to boil.

Mix the egg yolks and sugar together in a bowl until the mixture is rich and creamy.

Then pour the vanilla cream mixture slowly into the yolk and sugar mix, stirring well. Strain this through a sieve. Divide the mixture equally between 6 ramekins or other small ovenproof dishes.

Place the ramekins into a deep pan or roasting tin and add enough boiling water to come halfway up the sides of the dishes (to make a bain marie). Place this bain marie in the oven and bake for approximately 30–35 minutes, until the crème brûlées are set.

Allow to cool and then place in the fridge to chill completely.

To serve, sprinkle each with a thin, even layer of Demerara sugar and then glaze under a hot grill, or use a chef's blowtorch to caramelise the top of each crème brûlée. When it cools the sugar will set as a crisp thin crust.

*Per portion* *this dessert provides ½ a protein exchange.*

*While you don't usually think of desserts as having a lot of protein this recipe has the equivalent of about ½ an egg per portion and therefore it has been counted in the protein allowances for this recipe.*

*Check your daily allowances to see if you have enough remaining for this dessert.*

# Paul Flynn

## Quality, Just That

To many people, Dungarvan, Co. Waterford, may seem an unlikely centre for all that is good and great in Irish cuisine, but Paul Flynn and his team at the Tannery have created a Mecca for foodies – not just from Ireland but from around the globe. "It all boils down to one word, really: quality. It's in everything we do. At the Tannery, we pride ourselves on the fact that we work with the seasons; we only use ingredients that are fresh and local – follow this and you can't go wrong."

Paul's dishes are known and loved for their deep, earthy flavours. He prides himself on the simplicity of his menus and the knowledge that taste is what matters in the end. The Tannery has developed a network of small producers that provides the highest-quality ingredients, and these ingredients are the inspiration behind Paul's best-loved dishes. "Cooking with the best ingredients should be simple. The food should speak for itself – the less the chef has to do to the produce, the better."

Paul's cooking career started out in London with Nico Ladenis, working in his many restaurants. Paul was made head chef at the early age of 23 at Chez Nico in Great Portland

Street. He then went on to take charge of Chez Nico at Ninety Park Lane in the Grosvenor House Hotel, the current site of Richard Corrigan's restaurant in Mayfair. "We opened the Tannery in 1997 and today we also have the Tannery Cookery School and Garden. Opening the cookery school seemed like a natural progression, as more and more people are getting interested again in good food, not only cooking it but also learning about where it comes from."

At the Tannery Cookery School, Paul hosts cookery courses for everyone, from the amateur home cook to the more adventurous foodie and even those who might want to cook for a living. "It is very important to learn just what it takes to produce the food that a lot of us take for granted. I love the idea of planting seeds and watching my food grow. There is no better feeling for me than to wander around the garden collecting vegetables, then taking them to the kitchen, cooking and eating them – it's incredibly satisfying."

Paul's recipes for the cookbook reflect his philosophy when it comes to good food. "Start with the freshest, local, seasonal ingredients. If you remember these three words, you can't really go wrong. The main element is that you are about to create something that will not only be nourishing for your body but will lift your spirit as well: that's what good food is all about. I hope that my recipes will inspire you to try new things and perhaps make good food a part of your life, because, as the old saying goes, you are what you eat."

*The Tannery, 10 Quay Street, Dungarvan, Co. Waterford. Tel: 058 45420; www.tannery.ie*

* Please note the garnish in the photograph was included for illustration purposes only.

# Brandade of White Fish

**Serves 4**

2 tbsp olive oil
2 garlic cloves, sliced
1 small onion, sliced
200g (7oz) potatoes, peeled and diced
2 medium-sized fillets of fresh cod, skin removed and fish cut into chunks
125ml (4fl oz) milk
1 bay leaf
A pinch (¼ level tsp) freshly ground white pepper
Juice of ½ lemon
1 tbsp honey
2–3 tbsp extra-virgin olive oil
Warm pitta bread, to serve

Heat the olive oil in a stainless steel saucepan, add the garlic and fry over a low heat until it starts to turn golden. Add the sliced onions, cover with a lid and cook gently for 10 minutes or until softened.

Dice potatoes into 1cm (½in) cubes and cook in 10 times their volume of water until just tender. (See p. 282) Then drain and add to sliced onion mixture. Pour in enough milk to barely cover the mixture.

Add the cod and cook, stirring gently, until the cod is flaky and translucent. Purée the mixture with a hand blender or in a food processor. Slowly incorporate the extra-virgin olive oil whilst blitzing along with the pepper, honey and lemon juice. Do not over-process, as the consistency should be that of runny, lumpy, mashed potatoes. Spoon into a bowl.

Serve with warm pitta bread with a little extra-virgin olive oil drizzled on top.

 *This recipe is also suitable for fresh haddock, whiting, hake and plaice.*

 ***Per portion*** *this dish provides ½ a portion of vegetables, ½ a potato and 1½ protein exchanges.*

*If you have a daily allowance of dairy products, please note that there is milk in this recipe, which needs to be taken from your allowance.*

*Check your daily allowances to see if you have enough remaining for this dish.*

Paul Flynn

151

# Tuscan Lemon Chicken with Provencal Couscous

**Serves 4**

## FOR THE TUSCAN LEMON CHICKEN

I small chicken (approx. 3lb), jointed

150ml (5fl oz) olive oil

Zest of 2 lemons

150ml (5fl oz) fresh lemon juice

3 garlic cloves, finely chopped or grated

5 small sprigs (approx. 15g) fresh rosemary,
 finely chopped

A pinch (¼ level tsp) freshly ground black pepper

## FOR THE PROVENCAL COUSCOUS

300ml (½pt) chicken stock (add ½ a suitable chicken stock cube to 300ml water)

½ pinch ground turmeric

½ pinch paprika

½ pinch ground cumin

½ pinch chilli powder

½ pinch sugar

60ml (2fl oz) tomato juice

Juice of half an orange

175g (6oz) couscous

1 red onion, cut into 1cm (½in) cubes

1 tbsp olive oil

1 red pepper, halved, seeded and cut into 1cm (½in) cubes

½ yellow pepper, seeded and cut into 1cm (½in) cubes

1 garlic clove, crushed

100g (3½oz) courgette, trimmed and cut into 1cm (½in) cubes

A pinch (¼ level tsp) freshly ground black pepper

To prepare the chicken, mix the olive oil, lemon zest, lemon juice, garlic, rosemary and pepper in a bowl large enough to hold the chicken. Add the chicken pieces, turning to coat, and refrigerate, covered with clingfilm, for at least 2 hours or overnight ideally.

Preheat the oven to 180°C/350°F/Gas 4. Turn the chicken in the marinade once before cooking. Place the chicken on a baking tray in the oven and cook for 15 minutes. Turn over and cook for another 20–30 minutes until skin is golden brown. To check that the chicken pieces are cooked through, pierce the flesh with a skewer – if the juices run clear, then the chicken is cooked.

While the chicken is roasting you can prepare the couscous. Bring the stock, spices, tomato juice and orange juice to the boil and cook gently for 10 minutes. Pour the couscous into a large bowl and pour ¼ of the liquid over it. Stir, cover completely with clingfilm and allow to steam for 10 minutes. Break up with a fork and pour in another ¼ of the stock.

* Please note the garnish in the photograph was included for illustration purposes only.

Cover once more and let it rest for another 10 minutes. Again loosen with a fork. Add the rest of the stock to the couscous. Cover once more. Once the couscous has absorbed all the liquid and fluffed up, it is cooked. If you are left with any excess liquid after the couscous has fluffed up, you can simply drain it off.

Heat a large frying pan. Sauté the onion for 2–3 minutes in olive oil and then add peppers and garlic. Cook for 2 more minutes and then add in the courgette. Cook for a further 3–5 minutes or until the vegetables are tender but still holding their shape. Season with pepper and then mix the vegetables through the couscous.

When the chicken is cooked, remove it from the oven and allow it to rest for 10 minutes. Serve the chicken on warmed plates (allowing 150g per portion, weight includes skin) with a portion of Provençal couscous.

 *__Per portion__ this dish provides 1 portion of fruit, 2 portions of vegetables and 5 protein exchanges.*

*Do not use a homemade chicken stock. Ask your dietitian to suggest a suitable stock cube.*

*Check your daily allowances to see if you have enough remaining for this dish.*

# Tarte Tatin

**Serves 8**

90g (3¼oz) vanilla sugar
60g (2½oz) unsalted butter, cut into small chunks
8–10 crisp eating apples
Juice of 1 lemon
180g (6oz) puff pastry, thawed if frozen
Flour, for dusting
120ml (4fl oz) fresh cream, softly whipped, to serve

Preheat the oven to 180°C/350°F/Gas 4. Use a medium-sized ovenproof frying pan (as you will need to cook the tarte in the pan in the oven later). Put the sugar in the pan in a thin layer and heat it gently until it turns into a golden brown liquid and forms a caramel; do not let it burn. Once caramelised, remove from the heat and immediately add 20g butter, in small pieces, into the caramel. It will bubble instantly.

Peel and slice all the apples into quarters except one, which you should peel and cut in half, carefully removing the core with a teaspoon. Core the apples and sprinkle over some lemon juice to prevent them from discolouring. Put half an apple cut side up in the middle of the pan then place the quarters around it, tightly packed. Dot with the remaining 40g butter and place over a gentle heat, just to start the cooking process. Remove from the heat.

Roll out the pastry on a lightly floured surface and form it into a circle just bigger than the pan. Roll it loosely over the rolling pin and blanket the apples. Tuck the pastry down the side of the pan and bake in the oven for 25–30 minutes. Remove from the oven and leave to cool for 10 minutes. Cover the pan with a serving plate and invert the tarte on to it.

Serve with a small amount of softly whipped cream.

 *To make vanilla caster sugar, all you have to do is place a vanilla pod into a jar of caster sugar and allow to infuse for a few hours or as long as you can. You can purchase vanilla sugar in Tesco and M&S.*

 ***Per portion*** *this dessert provides 1 portion of fruit.*

*Check your daily allowances; to see if you have enough remaining for this dessert.*

Paul Flynn

# Paula McIntyre

Paula McIntyre

## *The Simpler the Cooking, the Better the Food*

Described by a recent radio-show host as the Kitchen Queen, Paula McIntyre certainly knows her food. "I started cooking with my mother when I was fourteen. I loved to bake. Some people that we knew opened a country house hotel, and it was there that I got my first taste, so to speak, of working in a professional kitchen."

After finishing school, Paula went on to train at the prestigious Johnson and Wales University of Culinary Arts in Rhode Island. "I had to fight to be allowed to follow a career in cooking – my career guidance teacher told me not to be so silly! But I was determined. I did hotel management in Belfast after I left school, and then I headed off to Rhode Island on a scholarship."

After leaving Belfast, Paula went to work at Michelin-starred L'Escargot in London. "That was a complete culture shock for me. I was used to working in a kitchen in a country guesthouse by the sea, where we could go outside into the fresh air for a break. I went from that to a basement kitchen in Soho, where the only daylight came in when the trap door opened as produce was delivered. It really focused the mind!"

156

Paula then set her heart on opening her own restaurant and, in 1993, she did just that in Manchester. "I think I always wanted my own place and when the chance came along I took it." After winning many awards in Manchester, Paula decided that it was time to return home to Ireland. "I took the job as head chef in Ghan House in Carlingford, but today I love teaching and that's what I spend much of my time doing these days."

Over the years, Paula has worked with many types of cooking but now knows that the simpler the cooking, the better the food. "I remember when I was training, it was all about showing off your technique. Now I like to let the ingredients be the stars of my cooking. This is something that we all need to get back to. My favourite food has to be seafood and I think that a good piece of fish, simply cooked with a butter sauce, is as good as any foam or other elaborate concoction that we see so much of these days. Keep it simple: that's the key to success with good food."

Paula enjoyed the challenge we set her for this recipe book. "I was really intrigued by the list of ingredients I was given. But when you get down to the bare facts, the challenge was really about knowing what is good for you and then making that special. Pick the freshest, local ingredients and, above all, enjoy your food."

*www.paulamcintyre.com*

# Za'atar Spiced Tuna with Creamed Cucumber Salad and Carrot and Ginger Dressing

**Serves 6**

## FOR THE ZA'ATAR SPICED TUNA

400g (14oz) fresh blue fin tuna,
  cut into 6 even lengths
1 level tbsp fresh oregano, chopped
Zest and juice of 1 lemon
  (retain the juice for the dressing)
½ level tsp paprika
½ level tsp ground coriander
½ level tsp ground cumin
1 tsp toasted sesame oil

## FOR THE CREAMED CUCUMBER

1 cucumber
2 spring onions, finely chopped
1 level tbsp fresh mint leaves, chopped
1 level tbsp fresh coriander, chopped
1 level tbsp crème fraîche

## FOR THE CARROT AND GINGER DRESSING

75g (3oz) carrots, peeled and sliced
5g (¼oz) root ginger, peeled and sliced
75ml (3fl oz) olive oil
Juice of 1 lemon
½ tsp honey

To make the Za'atar spiced tuna, mix everything together in a large bowl and cover and leave to marinate in the fridge for a few hours.

To make the creamed cucumber, peel the cucumber and split down the middle in half. Scoop out the seeds and discard. Chop the cucumber into ½cm (¼in) dice and mix it in a bowl with the other ingredients.

Preheat the oven to 200°C/400°F/Gas 6. To make the carrot and ginger dressing, toss the carrots and ginger in one teaspoon of the oil. Place in tinfoil, seal up and roast in the oven for 45 minutes or so until soft. Then place in a liquidiser and blend with the remaining oil, lemon juice and honey. Blend to a smooth purée and place in a squeezy bottle if you have one, or simply set aside in a small jug or glass.

When ready to cook the tuna, remove from the fridge 10 minutes before cooking. Then heat a pan until very hot and cook the tuna for 4–5 minutes on each side, until the fish

\* Please note the garnish in the photograph was included for illustration purposes only.

feels firm. Once cooked through, immediately remove the tuna pieces from the pan and set aside on a plate.

To serve, slice each piece of tuna into 3 pieces. Spoon 3 dollops of the cucumber onto a plate and top with tuna pieces. Drizzle over the dressing.

 **Per portion** *this dish provides 1 portion of vegetables and 2 protein exchanges.*
*Check your daily allowances to see if you have enough remaining for this dish.*

# Grilled Paillard of Chicken with Penne Pasta, Courgettes, Peppers and Mint

**Serves 4**

**FOR THE CHICKEN**
4 x 150g (5oz) skinless chicken breasts
1 level tsp fresh thyme, chopped
2 garlic cloves, crushed
Zest and juice of 1 lemon (keep the zest for later)
1 tbsp olive oil
A pinch (¼ level tsp) freshly ground black pepper

**FOR THE PENNE PASTA WITH COURGETTES, PEPPERS AND MINT**
250g (9oz) red peppers, seeded and sliced into strips
175g (6oz) penne pasta
1 tbsp olive oil
150g (5oz) courgettes, sliced
100g (3½oz) red onion, diced
1 garlic clove, chopped finely
100ml (3½fl oz) chicken stock (use an ⅛ of a suitable chicken stock cube to 100ml water)
15g (½oz) fresh mint leaves, chopped
Zest of 1 lemon, from above
1 level tbsp freshly grated Parmesan, made with pasteurised milk
15g (½oz) fresh parsley, chopped (for garnish)

To prepare the chicken, lay each chicken breast between two sheets of clingfilm and beat with a rolling pin to flatten. Mix all the other ingredients in a bowl and add the chicken breasts, turning to coat well. Cover the bowl with clingfilm and leave to marinate for a couple of hours.

Preheat the oven to 200°C/400°F/Gas 6. Coat the peppers in a little olive oil and then roast in an ovenproof dish for 15 minutes or until the skin is blistered but not burnt. Then let the peppers cool, peel them and chop them into dice. Set aside.

To cook the chicken, heat a griddle pan or frying pan until smoking hot. Season the chicken with a little pepper and place in the pan. Cook for at least 5 minutes on each side. Remove from the heat and cut into the centre of one of the chicken breasts to make sure it is

cooked through. If not, return the chicken to hot pan for a further 2–3 minutes.

To prepare the pasta, bring a large pot of water to the boil, add in the penne and cook for 10–12 minutes or so (follow the pasta packet instructions). Drain and set the pasta aside.

To prepare the vegetables, heat the oil in a large pan until hot and add the onion and garlic. Cook for 2 minutes. Then add the courgettes and cook for a further 2 minutes. Add the stock and then stir in the cooked pasta and add the chopped mint, zest of lemon and freshly grated parmesan.

Divide among warm plates and place a chicken breast on each. Garnish with fresh parsley.

 *Per portion* this dish provides 2 portions of vegetables and 5 protein exchanges.

*If you have a daily allowance of dairy products, please note that there is cheese in this recipe, which needs to be taken from your allowance.*

*Do not use a homemade chicken stock. Ask your dietitian to suggest a suitable stock cube.*

*Check your daily allowances to see if you have enough remaining for this dish.*

# Baked Plums with Blueberries and Orange and Vanilla Meringues (LF)

**Serves 4**

| | |
|---|---|
| 8 plums (not too ripe) | **FOR THE ORANGE AND VANILLA MERINGUES** |
| 75g (3oz) frozen blueberries | 3 egg whites |
| Zest and juice of 1 orange | 150g (5oz) caster sugar |
|    (keep some for the meringues) | ½ level tsp cornflour |
| 1 vanilla pod or a drop of | 1 tsp white wine vinegar |
|    vanilla extract | 2 tsp orange zest (from before) |
| 75g (3oz) caster sugar | Vanilla seeds from above, or a drop of vanilla extract |
| 1 tbsp honey | 50ml (2fl oz) natural yoghurt, for serving |

Preheat the oven to 180°C/350°F/Gas 4. Cut the plums in half, remove stones and place cut-side up in a baking dish.

Place the blueberries, orange juice, sugar and honey in a saucepan. Split the vanilla pod, scrape out the seeds and set aside, then add the empty pod to the ingredients in the pot. Or simply add in a drop of vanilla extract if you do not have a vanilla pod. Put the pot on a medium-high heat and let it boil for about 10 minutes, until it forms a thick syrup, stirring occasionally. Pour this syrup over the plums, cover with a piece of greaseproof paper and roast for 20 minutes or until soft, checking them throughout the cooking to make sure they do not burn.

To make the meringues, reduce the oven to 110°C/225°F/Gas ¼.
Line a baking sheet with non-stick parchment paper. Whisk the egg whites in a clean bowl until the mixture will hold a stiff peak. Keep whisking and slowly add the sugar. When fully incorporated, mix the cornflour and vinegar and add to the meringue mixture. Fold in the orange zest and vanilla seeds (or extract). Place in a piping bag and pipe on to the baking sheet – either in 4 round swirls or in cigar shapes. Bake for about 1 hour or until crisp on the outside and gooey inside. Turn off the oven and allow meringues to cool in the oven.

Arrange the meringues on plates and serve beside the baked plums with a tiny swirl of natural yoghurt.

 **Per portion** this dessert provides 2 portions of fruit.

*If you have a daily allowance of dairy products, please note that there is yoghurt in this recipe, which needs to be taken from your allowance.*

*Check your daily allowances to see if you have enough for this dessert.*

# Paula Mee

*Balance – It's All About Balance*

Dietitian and nutritional consultant Paula Mee is known for her no-nonsense, down-to-earth approach to food. Paula graduated from the National University of Ireland, Galway, with a BSc in biochemistry and then completed her postgraduate qualifications in dietetics and a master's in health science at Leeds Metropolitan University. "I found myself gravitating towards the nutrition section of my course and, after I left NUIG, I decided to concentrate on this. From here, cooking became a key part of my life and work; I find the physical act of cooking both nourishing and nurturing. I like nothing better than cooking up a batch of food for the freezer."

In 2004, Paula began her work as a nutritional consultant and, as part of her working week, she operates a dietetic and weight-management clinic in the Dublin Nutrition Centre. "I like foods with 'clean' flavours, as you find in many Asian cooking cultures. I also believe Mediterranean cuisine is one of the healthiest around."

Currently on the board of Consumer Foods for Bord Bía, Paula is well known as one of the presenters of RTÉ's *Health Squad* programme. "It seems like a long time ago now, but the show ran from 2002 until 2006. I think it is important to remember that it's what you eat *most of the time* that's important. We can't all be perfect every day, but if you really try to ensure the food you eat is balanced nutritionally most of the time, then you will feel better for it."

The message that Paula is keen to get across is that healthy food can taste great, as well as being good for you. "The problem is we have all been fooled into believing that we save time and money by using processed foods and ready meals, many of which are high in calories but low in nutrition. The real truth is that it's just a matter of stocking up on foods that don't take much time to prepare, but which will keep you going for longer and are better for your body. When we eat a lot of fast foods, we get more sugar, fat and salt but very little nourishment to sustain us. We feel hungrier sooner and end up eating more than we need as a result.

"My recipes in this book are all easy to make, look great on the plate and have a good balance of protein, fats and carbohydrates – they also deliver a lot of vitamins and minerals. My advice is to have confidence and enjoy your cooking, be open to trying new things and remember, if you eat well, you will feel well. Use good ingredients and enjoy eating good food every day. I found putting the recipes together for this book challenging – the challenge was all about the quantity and quality of the ingredients that could be used. I hope that you will enjoy cooking and eating my meals."

*www.paulamee.com*

# Roasted Pepper Tarts

**Serves 4**

2 red peppers
4 sheets filo pastry (30 x 20cm/11 x 8in)
1 egg white, beaten
15g (½oz) fresh basil leaves, torn
2 level tbsp tomato passata, available in the Italian section of all
   good supermarkets and delis
A pinch (¼ level tsp) freshly ground black pepper
60g (2oz) cherry tomatoes, to garnish

4 x non-stick individual tartlet tins, 10cm (4in) in diameter.

Preheat the oven to 190°C/375°F/Gas 5. Cut the peppers in half, remove the seeds and place them cut-side down on a non-stick baking sheet. Roast in the oven for 20 minutes or until soft. Remove from the oven and place inside a plastic food bag. Seal the bag and leave to cool. Peel the cooled peppers and roughly chop.

Stack the filo pastry sheets on top of each other. Using a scissors cut the stack into 4 equal square sections so that you end up with 16 individual squares.

In each tartlet tin, place 4 individual pastry squares in layers, placing the squares at slight right angles to each other and brushing with beaten egg white between each layer.

Bake in the oven for 8–10 minutes until crisp and golden brown. Allow to cool and carefully remove from the tins.

To make the filling, combine the chopped peppers with some torn basil and the passata in a bowl. Spoon the mixture into the baked shells and return to the oven to warm through.

Garnish each tart with a cherry tomato cut in half and the torn basil leaves.
Serve warm on plates.

*These simple tarts will really impress your dinner party guests!*
*They look divine and you can have them ready to assemble well in advance.*

*Per portion this recipe provides 1½ portions of vegetables.*

*Check your daily allowances to see if you have enough remaining for this dish.*

# Lamb Kebabs and Basmati Rice

**Serves 4**

### FOR THE KEBABS

400g (14oz) lamb, cut into 2.5cm (1in) cubes
1 large red onion, peeled
1 large green pepper

### FOR THE BASMATI RICE

275g (10oz) basmati rice
2 level tbsp fresh coriander, chopped (optional)
1 tbsp olive oil
600ml (1pt) boiling water

### FOR THE MARINADE

1 tbsp olive oil
½ level tsp ground cumin
½ level tsp dried oregano
½ level tsp ground ginger
½ level tsp ground cinnamon
Juice of half an orange (28ml/1fl oz)
1 level tbsp fresh coriander, chopped
1 tbsp clear honey

Mix all of the marinade ingredients together in a bowl. Stir in the lamb and cover with clingfilm. Leave to marinate for 1–2 hours in the fridge. Meanwhile, soak 8 wooden skewers in water.

Cut each onion half into 4 equal wedges and remove the white core from each piece. Split the wedges in half to make 16 thin pieces of onion. Cut the pepper in half and remove the core and the seeds, then cut the pepper into 16 even-sized pieces (similar in size to the onion chunks).

Remove the skewers from the water and place a cube of lamb on a skewer, followed by pieces of onion and pepper. Repeat and add a piece of lamb to finish. Do the same for all 8 skewers.

Preheat the grill to a medium heat. Grill the kebabs for 12–15 minutes, turning every 2–3 minutes. Once cooked, allow to rest for a few minutes before serving.

While the kebabs are cooking, prepare the rice. Place the olive oil in a saucepan on a medium heat. Add in basmati rice and turn the grains over until they are nicely coated and glistening with oil. Pour the boiling water on to the rice, stir once and cover with lid. Turn the heat down to its lowest setting and let the rice cook for exactly 15 minutes. Do not take the lid off at any stage. Now take the pan off the heat, remove the lid and cover with a clean tea cloth for 5 minutes. Before serving, fluff up rice with a fork and add in the chopped coriander (if using).

To serve, arrange the lamb kebabs on warmed plates with the basmati rice.

 *Per portion this dish provides 1 portion of vegetables and 3 protein exchanges.*

*Check your daily allowances to see if you have enough remaining for this dish.*

* Please note the garnish in the photograph was included for illustration purposes only.

# Easy Baked Pears

**Serves 4**

4 ripe pears
4 level tbsp reduced-fat crème fraîche
½ level tsp ground cinnamon
4 tbsp clear honey
8 gingernut biscuits

Preheat the oven to 190°C/375°F/Gas 5. Cut each pear in half, then place them cut-side up on a large baking sheet. Use a teaspoon to scoop out the cores and make a dip in the centre of each one. Sprinkle over the cinnamon and drizzle with a little honey.

Roast the pears in the oven for 10–15 minutes. Meanwhile, put the biscuits into a food bag and use a rolling pin to crush them lightly. Remove the pears from the oven, then put a tablespoon of reduced-fat crème fraîche in the dip of each pear. Scatter the biscuit crumbs over each pear to serve.

 ***Per portion*** *this dessert provides 1½ portions of fruit.*

*Check your daily allowances to see if you have enough remaining for this dessert.*

# Peter Merrigan

## It's All About the Quality

From the Hilton Hotel to the high seas, head chef for the Avoca Group Peter Merrigan has his grandmother to thank for his love of food. Peter's grandmother owned and ran a bakery in Bray, Co. Wicklow, and, although he never worked in the bakery, Peter always knew he wanted to work with food. "I remember the smells that used to come from the bakery and, when I left school, I knew that there was only one thing I wanted to do – and that was cook. So my first job in a kitchen was at the Hilton Hotel in Charlemont Place, Dublin."

There, Peter honed his skills and was educated on the basics of food preparation; he learned about taste and how important it was to have good ingredients. "In a hotel kitchen, you learn very quickly as you are transferred around from section to section. I saw how to prepare everything from a banquet for three hundred people down to fine dining for fifty, but there was one constant: no matter how many people you needed to feed, it all boiled down to the quality of the ingredients."

Next, Peter took his newfound culinary skills on to a cruise ship, sailing across the blue waters of the Caribbean. "The cruise ship was like a huge floating hotel. It had five different-style restaurants, serving everything from hamburgers to foie gras. It was a fantastic experience and very hard work. On board the ship, life was extremely regimented. We had big, white hats and pristine uniforms that were pressed every day – it was like being in the navy, really."

So, after all his varied food experiences, what is Peter's abiding food philosophy? "I like to keep things simple. A good dish doesn't need lots of ingredients, just a few well-chosen ones – that's all you need. Here in Avoca, we demand the best quality when it comes to our ingredients and I know it shows. I like to think my style is all about fresh, healthy, clean food. I love Italian foods, from cured meats and salads to simple pasta dishes. When I'm not at work, I love to make pasta and, to be honest, you can't beat your own mother's cooking. When I go home, I love nothing better than my mother's Irish stew."

For this book, Peter created recipes with his personal food philosophy in mind. "If I had only two ingredients in my kitchen, they would have to be onions and garlic. These two ingredients can add so much flavour and goodness to dishes – I would find it hard not to have them about. When I saw the list of ingredients, I found it very interesting. Certain bits and pieces that, as a chef, I would have used without really thinking, I suddenly had to find alternatives for. But I found that the challenge made me rethink some of my methods, which was really good for me. I really enjoyed the whole experience, and I hope that you have fun using my recipes. Remember, cooking is all about enjoying yourself. Take your time, make mistakes – you can start again, but always use good ingredients."

*Avoca Rathcoole, Fitzmaurice Road, Rathcoole, Co. Dublin. Tel: 01 2571800.*

# Spiced Carrot and Pumpkin Soup

**Serves 6**

50g (2oz) butter
240g (8½oz) Spanish onion, finely diced
3 garlic cloves
¼ red chilli, 4g (⅛oz) seeded and chopped
A pinch (¼ level tsp) ground cumin
1 level tsp ground coriander
1 level tsp fresh thyme, chopped finely
135g (4½oz) leek, sliced
225g (8oz) carrot, peeled and chopped

200g (7oz) pumpkin flesh, seeded
    and chopped
900ml (1½pt) water
80g (3oz) Parmesan, made with
    pasteurised milk, freshly grated
100ml (3½fl oz) cream
A pinch (¼ level tsp) freshly ground
    black pepper

Place a large casserole pot or deep pot on a medium heat and melt the butter. Add the onion, garlic, chilli, spices and thyme to the pan. Reduce the heat and cover the pan with a lid to allow the vegetables to sweat for 5 minutes without browning. Then remove the lid, add the leek and cook for a further 5 minutes, stirring occasionally.

Add the carrots and pumpkin to the pot and cover with the water. Reduce the heat to a simmer and let the contents simmer gently for 45–50 minutes, until the vegetables are completely soft.

Remove from the heat and blitz the contents of the pot with a handheld blender (or use a food processor). Add in the Parmesan cheese and cream and season with black pepper to taste.

Ladle into warmed bowls to serve.

*When making soup, you don't want to make it too thin, so it is a good tip to reserve some of your stock and only add it in after you have blitzed the soup to thin the mixture if necessary. Remember, you can always add more liquid to thin a soup but it is much harder to thicken it.*

***Per portion** this dish provides 2 portions of vegetables and 1 dairy exchange.*

*If you are on a fluid restriction, remember to count this soup as part of your daily intake.*

*Check your daily allowances to see if you have enough remaining for this dish.*

# Tagliatelle Pasta with Poached Fresh Salmon and Dill Cream

**Serves 4**

150g (5oz) tagliatelle pasta
300g (10oz) fresh salmon
½ a lemon
150g (5oz) asparagus spears
100g (3½oz) cucumber, cut into
ribbons, to garnish

100g (3½oz) broccoli florets
Juice of 1 lime
100g (3½oz) crème fraîche
1 level tbsp fresh dill, chopped
A pinch (¼ level tsp) freshly ground black pepper

Bring a large pot of water to the boil. Add the tagliatelle pasta and cook as per packet instructions, stirring regularly to prevent the pasta from sticking. Once cooked, drain and then run cold water over the pasta to cool it and stop it from cooking any further. Set aside.

To poach the salmon, place the salmon in a pot of slightly boiling water, add the half lemon and dill to the water and poach for 7–9 minutes, until the flesh of the fish has turned pale and opaque. Remove the salmon from the pot and leave it to cool.

Blanch the asparagus and broccoli by parboiling them in boiling water for 4–6 minutes, then drain and run them under cold water to stop the cooking process.

Place the olive oil in a generous pan, add the asparagus spears and broccoli florets and pan-fry slightly. Next add the cooked tagliatelle and crème fraîche and mix well. Flake the poached salmon into the pasta trying to keep it a little chunky. Then add in the lime juice and chopped dill and mix. Remove the dish from heat, and season with black pepper.

To prepare the cucumber, use a vegetable peeler to peel it lengthways and make nice cucumber ribbons.

Serve the pasta in warm bowls with cucumber ribbons on top.

 *Per portion* this dish provides 1½ portions of vegetables and 2 protein exchanges. *Check your daily allowances to see if you have enough remaining for this dish.*

* Please note the garnish in the photograph was included for illustration purposes only.

# Fluffy American Pancakes with Mixed Berries and Yoghurt

**Serves 6**

115g (4oz) plain flour
25g (1oz) cornflour
½ level tbsp bread soda
A tiny pinch of ground cinnamon
25g (1oz) caster sugar
200ml (7fl oz) milk
1 egg

¼ vanilla pod, seeds scraped out
Butter, for greasing
100g (3½oz) mixed berries, such as raspberries,
   strawberries and blueberries
25ml (1fl oz) maple syrup
50ml (2fl oz) Greek-style yoghurt
Icing sugar, to decorate

To make the pancakes, sift the flour, cornflour, bread soda and ground cinnamon into a bowl, then add in the caster sugar and mix well. In a separate bowl, whisk the milk, eggs and vanilla seeds together until well mixed.

Make a well in the centre of the dry ingredients and pour the blended milk mixture into the well. Whisk the liquid, bringing the dry ingredients into the liquid as you go. Whisk until the batter is silky smooth and all the dry ingredients have been incorporated. Cover the bowl and leave mixture to rest for one hour.

Heat a large frying pan on a moderate heat, add a knob of butter and let it melt. Add enough batter to the pan to form a circle about 7.5cm (3in) in diameter.

The pancake might look a little bit thick but let it cook on a low heat until bubbles start forming on top of the pancake. Then turn it and cook for a further 3 minutes on the other side. You should fit 2–3 pancakes in a large frying pan. You will need to make 6 in total. If you like your berries warm, heat them up gently in a small pot with a little bit of maple syrup, or else just serve them plain.

Serve each pancake with berries and yoghurt on the side. Pour over a little maple syrup and decorate with a sprinkling of icing sugar.

 **Per portion** *this dessert provides ½ a portion of fruit.*

*If you have a daily allowance of dairy products, please note that there is yoghurt and milk in this recipe which needs to be taken from your allowance.*

*Check your daily allowances to see if you have enough remaining for this dish.*

# Rachel Allen

## Food or Shoes?

Before Rachel Allen arrived at the famous Ballymaloe cookery school, food was never high on her agenda. "I loved baking when I was growing up but I wasn't one of those children who knew what I wanted to do from an early age. It was when I arrived at Ballymaloe on the first day and Darina (Allen) gave her welcome talk that I realised this was for me." However, when Rachel finished her course at Ballymaloe she did toy with the idea of going into shoe design. "For a while all I wanted to do was cook but then every so often I would think about designing shoes or opening a shoe shop. It was an idea that had been going around in my head for years. So I found myself making a final choice – food or shoes?"

Well, shoe design missed out and Rachel is now a world-famous chef, cookery writer, TV presenter and good food champion. "Good food is hugely important to me, for myself and for my family. For me, good food is essential to good health. We are all affected by the food we consume so it is imperative to put some serious thought into what and how we eat. Of course, cooking and eating should also be fun." For Rachel the act of cooking is only one part of the process of eating good food. "Shopping is key. Be governed by the seasons. I know it sounds boring but seasonal eating is so important; it's better for flavour and for cost too. I stay away from processed foods as much as I can; fresh food is so much better for your body and you will feel the benefits almost immediately. Get in touch with the people in your community who can help you source good food. For example, your neighbourhood butcher, he or she can advise you on how to prepare cuts of meat that you might never have used before. I would like to see more people supporting their local butchers, bakers and greengrocers – that's where you will find the best food in every community."

Rachel's recipes in this book are examples of her love of unfussy, tasty food. "The list of ingredients that I was given to work from for the book didn't pose to much of a challenge for me. I think the renal diet, although restricted, offers plenty of choice to produce good tasty food. The main point to remember is to enjoy the whole process, get the best ingredients you can and above all have fun with your food."

*www.rachelallen.co.uk*

# Watermelon Salad with Marinated Irish Cheddar, Lime and Mint

**Serves 4**

350g (12oz) watermelon flesh
Zest and Juice of 1 lime
1 level tsp fresh mint, chopped
110g (4oz) Irish cheddar, made with pasteurised milk, cut into 1.5cm (½in) cubes

**FOR THE MARINADE**
2 tbsp grape seed oil
1 clove of garlic, halved
1 sprig of fresh rosemary

To make the marinade, combine the grape seed oil, garlic and sprig of rosemary in a bowl and then add the cubes of Irish cheddar. Mix well. Cover and allow to marinate for 8 hours or overnight.

Cut the watermelon into quarters and remove the seeds then chop the flesh into 2cm (¾in) pieces. Place in a bowl and add the marinated cheese, finely grated zest and juice of the lime, and the mint. Toss gently and serve as soon as possible, best served within an hour or so of making.

 *Per portion* this dish provides 1 portion fruit and 1 dairy exchange.

*Check your daily allowances to see if you have enough remaining for this dish.*

# Spicy Lamb Meatballs with Greek Salad and Mint Yoghurt

**Serves 6**

### FOR SPICY LAMB MEATBALLS

450g (1lb) minced lamb

1 level tsp ground cumin

1 level tsp ground coriander

3 green cardamom pods,
   split open and extract the seeds

4 garlic cloves, crushed or grated

1 small egg, beaten

2 tbsp olive oil

A pinch (¼ level tsp) freshly ground
   black pepper

### FOR THE MINT YOGHURT

250g (9oz) thick Greek yoghurt

1 level tbsp fresh mint, chopped

Juice of half a lemon

A pinch (¼ level tsp) freshly ground black pepper

### FOR THE GREEK GREEN SALAD

225g (8oz) mixed green salad leaves, washed
   (may include butterhead, boston, bibb, webb, cos,
   romaine, iceberg, red leaf and rocket. Avoid spinach
   leaves.)

1 small red onion, finely sliced or 3–4 spring onions, sliced

½ fresh cucumber, cut into 2cm (¾in) chunks

15g (½oz) fresh dill, chopped roughly

3 tbsp extra-virgin olive oil

¼ tbsp freshly squeezed lemon juice

1 level tbsp fresh parsley, chopped

A pinch (¼ level tsp) freshly ground black pepper

A pinch (¼ level tsp) sugar

Preheat the oven to 230°C/450°F/Gas 8.

To make the meatballs, mix all the ingredients except the olive oil together. With slightly wet hands, make little balls, slightly smaller than a walnut shell – about 2cm (¾in) diameter. This amount should make 25–30 meatballs.

Heat up the olive oil in a frying pan, add the meatballs and toss over high heat to brown, then transfer into a roasting tin and finish in the oven.

While the meatballs are cooking, make the salad. Place the mixed green salad leaves in a wide bowl with the fresh dill, cucumber and onions. Make the dressing in a small bowl; mix the olive oil, lemon juice, parsley, and season with the black pepper and a pinch of sugar. Drizzle the dressing over the salad.

When the meatballs are cooked, split one open to check that it's fully cooked. If it is not, return the meatballs to the hot oven for a further 2–3 minutes.

To serve, make a bed on each plate with the Greek green salad, top with 4–5 meatballs and then dress with the yoghurt dressing. Serve with white crusty bread.

 *These mini meatballs are also great to serve at a party (kids love them). Try serving them on a plate with a cocktail stick stuck in each one and a bowl of mint yoghurt in the centre.*

 ***Per portion*** *this dish provides 1½ portions of vegetables, 2½ protein exchanges and ½ a dairy exchange.*

*Check your daily allowances to see if you have enough remaining for this dish.*

# Pavlova with Passion Fruit and Kiwi

**Serves 8**

3 egg whites
350g (12oz) caster sugar
60ml (2fl oz) hot water
1 tsp white wine vinegar
1 level tsp cornflour
½ tsp vanilla extract

**TO SERVE**
200ml (7fl oz) cream
3 kiwi fruit, peeled
2 passion fruit

Preheat the oven to 200°C/400°F/Gas 6. Place a sheet of parchment paper on a baking sheet.

Beat all the meringue ingredients in an electric food mixer or with a hand mixer at a high speed for 5 minutes or until the mixture is stiff. Spread the mixture out on the parchment paper in a circle about 30cm (12in) in diameter and about 3–4cm (1¼–1½in) thick, making a wide, shallow well in the centre (for the cream and the fruit to sit in when serving).

Place in the oven, then immediately turn it off and leave the meringue to cook slowly for at least 5 hours or overnight.

Carefully transfer the cooked and cooled meringue to a large serving plate. Whip the cream softly and spread over the top of the meringue. Remove the skin from the kiwi fruit and slice, then lay slices on top of the cream. Cut the passion fruit in half and using a teaspoon scoop out the pulp, then drizzle over the kiwi. Serve the same day.

 *The meringue needs to stay in the oven for a very long time after cooking, so be sure to plan any other cooking you may need to do accordingly.*

 *Per portion this dessert provides ½ a portion of fruit.*

*Check your daily allowances to see if you have enough remaining for this dessert.*

# Richie Wilson

## *You Don't Get a Dog and Bark Yourself*

Richie Wilson always wanted to be a chef. In fact, as a child, Richie would play at being a chef with his mother and grandmother in the kitchen. "I never wanted to be a fireman or a pilot – I just wanted to cook. The kitchen was always the place I wanted to be."

This desire to be a chef stayed with Richie right through his school years, so much so that he wanted to finish school early to follow his dream. "I just wanted to leave school and get cooking but, looking back on it now, I am glad that I finished with my Leaving Cert."

Richie's first job in a kitchen was in Dublin's Gresham Hotel. "I started off as the lowest of the low in the kitchen at the Gresham that summer. But I still fell in love with it all and I knew for sure that I had made the right decision. I enrolled with CERT and headed off to Athlone to do my training."

Richie finished his training and went on to achieve the highest points in Ireland that year. "After that, I got a scholarship to train in America and I worked for a while in Rhode Island. When I returned to Ireland, I cooked in the Hibernian Hotel in Dublin. Then, one day, I got a call from Paul Flynn at the Tannery and I went to work with him in Dungarvan."

Richie learned a lot from Paul Flynn before moving on to the bright lights and twinkling Michelin star of Kevin Thornton's kitchen. "I worked for Kevin for three years and it was amazing. Life in that kitchen was very, very tough. When I started, Kevin already had one Michelin star, and I will always remember the day that Thornton's was awarded a second star – it was unbelievable."

After Thornton's, Richie came full circle and returned to work in the kitchen of a top-class hotel. "I was twenty-four when I took the job as sous chef in the Westin Hotel. As part of the executive team, I was responsible for twenty-three chefs, the budgets and keeping up with deadlines. I was glad I'd finished school."

Now Richie is executive head chef at the Morrison Hotel and describes his food as seasonal with a modern Irish touch. "Our food at the Morrison may sound very traditional, but we use only the best Irish ingredients we can get.

At home, Richie somehow still finds time to cook for his family. "I do most of the cooking at home. My wife often says that 'you don't get a dog and bark yourself', so, on the rare occasions that she does cook, it's a real treat for me. I hope you enjoy my recipes in this book – cooking is all about trying new things. Enjoy the whole experience but, most of all, enjoy your food!"

*Halo Restaurant, The Morrison Hotel, Ormond Quay, Dublin 1.*
*Tel: 01 8872400; www.morrisonhotel.ie*

# Scotch Broth

**Serves 6**

**FOR THE SCOTCH BROTH**

500g (18oz) diced mutton or lamb, trimmed and diced
1.5 litre (2½ pt) chicken stock (use only 1 suitable chicken stock cube to 1500ml water)
100g (3½oz) pearl barley
100g (3½oz) carrot, peeled and diced
50g (2oz) leek, trimmed and diced
50g (2oz) turnip, diced
100g (3½oz) cabbage, shredded
20g (¾oz) fresh parsley, chopped

To make the soup, it's a good idea to place the lamb/mutton in a pot of cold water and bring it to the boil. Remove it from the heat immediately and rinse the meat under cold running water. This will remove any blood or impurities from the meat.

Place the meat in a large clean pot and add the chicken stock and then the pearl barley. Bring this to the boil and reduce to a simmer and cook for a further 50 minutes. Now add the carrot, leek and turnip, stirring to combine. Continue to simmer for another 20 minutes or so until the carrots are almost tender. Add the cabbage and cook for another 10 minutes until the lamb and vegetables are all completely tender.

Just before serving, use a large spoon to remove any excess fat from the top of the pot. Add the chopped parsley and serve in piping hot bowls. You can almost feel this soup doing you good as you eat it. It's like a huge hug in a mug!

***Per portion*** *this dish provides 1 portion of vegetables and 2½ protein exchanges.*

*Do not use a homemade chicken stock. Ask your dietitian to suggest a suitable stock cube. If you need to restrict your daily fluid intake, remember to count this broth as part of your daily fluid allowance.*

*Check your daily allowances to see if you have enough remaining for this dish.*

Richie Wilson

# Barbecued Leg of Lamb with Rosemary Marinade, Lacour Potatoes and Summer Salad

**Serves 6**

**FOR THE LAMB**

1.1kg boneless leg of lamb, butterflied
(you can ask your butcher to do this for you)

**FOR THE MARINADE**

2 garlic cloves, peeled
1 level tsp fresh thyme
1 level tsp fresh rosemary
250ml (9fl oz) white wine
A pinch (¼ level tsp) freshly ground black pepper

**FOR THE LACOUR POTATOES**

1.2kg (2lbs 10oz) potatoes (Roosters work best)
Vegetable oil, for deep-fat frying
1 tbsp olive oil
1 garlic clove, finely chopped
4 shallots, finely chopped
1 level tsp fresh thyme, chopped
1 level tsp fresh parsley, chopped

**FOR THE SUMMER SALAD**

250g (9oz) mixed leaves (suitable
leaves include butterhead, boston, bibb,
webb, cos, romaine, iceberg, red leaf
and rocket. Avoid spinach.)
100g (3½oz) runner beans, topped and tailed
1 level tsp fresh coriander, chopped
1 level tsp fresh parsley, chopped
100g (3½oz) cherry tomatoes
50g (2oz) chopped spring onions
20ml (1½ tbsp) olive oil
Juice of 1 lemon

To prepare the marinade, simply add all the ingredients into a blender (or use a hand blender) and blend until all the herbs have been mixed through the wine. Place the butterflied leg of lamb in a roasting dish or similar and pour over the marinade, cover the meat well and leave for a maximum of 2 hours. If you are preparing this in advance, it's important to remove the lamb from the marinade after 2 hours or the flavours will get very strong and overpowering.

\* Please note the garnish in the photograph was included for illustration purposes only.

To cook the lamb keep the barbecue at a medium temperature in order to get the heat through the leg before the outside begins to char, continuously turn the leg throughout cooking and have a spray bottle of water to hand to quench any flames from dripping fat. The leg should take 60 to 80 minutes to cook. Cut into the meat to check that it is thoroughly cooked through to well done. Leave the meat to rest for a few minutes before carving.

Alternatively place in a preheated oven at 200°C/400°F/Gas 6 for 10 minutes and then reduce the temperature of the oven to 160°C/315°F/Gas 2½ and cook for a further 60 minutes.

To prepare the Lacour potatoes, peel the potatoes and dice into 1cm (½in) cubes. (see p. 282) Bring to the boil in 10 times their volume of water. Once they are soft, cool immediately in cold water. Strain and gently dry off the potatoes with a little kitchen paper. Now deep-fry them in a very hot deep-fat fryer (or wok or other large pot of oil) until golden. In a separate pot, heat the olive oil and fry the garlic, shallots, and thyme. While the pot is warm add the fried potatoes and turn them so as to mix them well with the other ingredients, but be careful not to break them up. Place a lid on top and allow them to sit for 5 minutes to soak up all the juices. When ready to serve sprinkle with the freshly chopped parsley.

It is possible to fry the potatoes beforehand and bring them to your barbecue but remember they will take a little longer to reheat in the pot.

To make the summer salad, firstly ensure that the leaves are fresh, washed and dry. Blanch the beans in hot water for no more than 2 minutes and immediately place in cool water; strain well before adding to the leaves. Put all the remaining ingredients in a salad bowl except the oil and lemon. Sprinkle the lemon over followed by the oil. Toss lightly and serve.

The best way to serve barbecued food is to let everyone help themselves, so keep it casual and serve the lamb in slices arranged on a plate or a big wooden board. Serve the potatoes in a large warm bowl with the salad alongside. Combine all this with a hot summer's day and you have barbecue bliss. Enjoy!

 *A butterflied leg of lamb is one that has been cut open and the meat unfolded, away from the bone, like a butterfly. When the resulting butterflied leg of lamb is laid flat, you get a thinner piece of meat, which will shorten the required cooking time. You will also increase the effectiveness of a marinade or dry rub since there will be more meat surface to absorb the flavours. You can ask your butcher to butterfly a leg of lamb for you.*

 ***Per portion*** *this dish provides 2 vegetable portions, 2 potatoes and 4½ protein exchanges.*

*Check your daily allowances to see if you have enough remaining for this dish.*

# Vanilla Pannacotta with Poached Pears

**Serves 4**

## FOR THE PANNACOTTA

3 gelatine leaves (10.5g)
1 vanilla pod
375ml (13fl oz) milk
275g (9½oz) cream
100g (3½oz) caster sugar

4 x 200ml (7fl oz) moulds

## FOR THE POACHED PEARS

4 small pears
50g (2oz) sugar
300ml (10½fl oz) water (enough to cover the pears)
1 level tsp ground cinnamon
2 whole cloves
100g (3½oz) fresh blueberries

To make the pannacotta, firstly soak the gelatine leaves in some cold water until ready to use.

Remove the seeds from the vanilla pod and set to one side, now place the remainder of the pod into a pot along with the milk and cream. Bring this gently to the boil and set to one side for 5–10 minutes before removing the vanilla pod. Now add the sugar to the pot along with the vanilla seeds. Return the pot to the heat and simmer until the sugar has dissolved, stirring all the while.

Now add the strained gelatine to the pot and stir until dissolved. It's a good idea to strain the mixture through a fine sieve or muslin cloth at this point to make sure there are no lumps before placing in the moulds. I think it's a good idea to find some slightly unusually shaped moulds for presentation purposes. I find the rubber moulds the best and choosing a pyramid shape or something similar will leave your guests wondering how you managed to get it that shape when they are so delicate. But here's how: simply fill these moulds with the pannacotta mixture and place on a tray. Once they have cooled sufficiently, place in the freezer. On the day you wish to serve them, remove them from the freezer and immediately push the pannacotta from the mould, placing them directly into the dish you wish to serve them in and allowing them to defrost there. Allow at least one hour at room temperature for them to defrost. Once you have placed them on the dish, there should be no reason to move them again and so they should keep their shape perfectly.

To poach the pears, firstly peel them, taking care to follow the natural contours of the pear so that when you're finished it still resembles a pear! Try to avoid removing the stalk from the top as it both looks good and helps to hold the pear together a little later on. Now, use an apple corer and press it through the bottom of the pear, as you would do with an

* Please note the garnish in the photograph was included for illustration purposes only.

apple, but do not push it through all the way. Remove the corer but don't worry about removing the core itself at this point, it will be much easier once the pear is poached. Now place all the remaining ingredients into a pot and bring to a simmer before adding the pears. Cover with some parchment paper and simmer gently for 10 minutes. Allow the pears to cool in the liquid.

Now with each pear, place it on a chopping board and hold the stalk in one hand. Using a knife, with the other hand, prize the core from the opposite end. It should come away very easily.

To present the dish, a nice wide-based bowl is best. Slice each pear, beginning 1cm or so below the stalk, all the way through and all the way to the bottom. Repeat this around the pear 4–5 times. Once this is done, you can press down gently on the pear and it should fan out leaving the stalk at the top holding it together. Place the pear alongside the pannacotta in the bowl and spoon a little of the poaching liquid over them both.

 **Per portion** *this dessert provides 1½ portions of fruit and ½ a dairy exchange.*

*Check your daily allowances to see if you have enough remaining for this dessert.*

# Rory O'Connell

Rory O'Connell

## Good Food is Health Food

Some people find their passion in life by accident. Rory O'Connell discovered his passion when he fell into a job at one of Ireland's top country house hotels. "I arrived at Ballymaloe House and was given the job of receptionist. Once I settled in, I realised that it was not the hotel side of the business I was interested in – I just wanted to learn how to cook good food."

Rory, brother of internationally renowned chef Darina Allen, began his love affair with good food as he trained at Ballymaloe with the woman who started it all, the wonderful Myrtle Allen. "I had eaten at Ballymaloe many times and there were certain dishes I wanted to learn how to make, simply because they tasted so good. My motivation was very selfish, actually!"

Today, Rory combines his passion for food with a love of teaching at his home in Shanagarry, Co. Cork. At the Ballymaloe Cookery School, we have a hundred acres of certified organic land, so we produce an awful lot of our own fruit and vegetables. This has become part of the way we teach people how to cook." In fact, Rory has taken this approach to another level. "When I give a cookery class in my home, or at Ballymaloe, the first thing I like to do is to get people out into the garden. They get their hands dirty and see how the food they are about to prepare is grown. It's important for people to realise that all food does not come from a supermarket, washed and wrapped in plastic.

Rory grew up in Cullahill, Co. Laois. "My mother was a great cook and we had our little plot of land where we grew vegetables, so I could see the food growing and eat the same food from our own garden. This is something I think everybody should try to experience for themselves. I get just as excited about a new Ballycotton potato today as I did thirty years ago."

When we set Rory the challenge to come up with recipes for this book, we knew he would rustle up something unpretentious and delicious. "When I got the list of ingredients, I saw no difficulty in coming up with exciting meals. I would say to anyone who is going to try my recipes, the first step is good shopping. There are a multitude of farmers' markets and local suppliers out there, so you don't have to go to the supermarkets for everything. It's also very important to shop seasonally, as this will make a real difference to your cooking. Then think about balance.

"I wanted my recipes to look good and taste good so that they make people feel good. This is very important. Good food is health food, and cooking can be very healing for both the cook and the diner. So, read the recipes from start to finish. Shop well to get the best-quality ingredients possible. When you return home, lay out all the ingredients, get yourself organised and just enjoy the whole process. Then all you need is someone to share it with."

*Snugboro, Ballybraher, Ballycotton, Co. Cork; www.rgoconnell.com*
*Ballymaloe Cookery School, Shanagarry, Co. Cork. Tel: 021 4646785.*

# Courgette Carpaccio with Rocket and Parmesan

**Serves 4**

200g (7oz) courgettes, yellow and green
80g (3oz) fresh rocket leaves
2 tbsp extra-virgin olive oil
Juice of 1 lemon
A pinch (¼ level tsp) of freshly ground black pepper
50g (2oz) Parmesan cheese made with pasteurised milk, shaved

Slice the courgettes very thinly, about 2mm (⅛in) thick, discarding the ends.
Dress with olive oil, lemon juice and pepper. The courgettes should be just glazed with
the oil. Do not end up with a pool of oil in the bottom of the bowl or it will go to waste.
Taste and correct the seasoning. Arrange the rocket leaves in a single layer on 4 flat
plates. Scatter the courgettes over the rocket, again in a single layer. Finally scatter
over the Parmesan and serve immediately.

 *This delicious summer salad is simple, but is dependent on the very best-quality
ingredients. Very small and fresh courgettes and peppery rocket leaves are
required. Best quality olive oil is also called for and if possible an organic lemon.*

 ***Per portion*** *this dish provides 2 portions of vegetables and ½ a dairy exchange.*

*Check your daily allowances to see if you have enough remaining for this dish.*

# Chicken with Leeks and Tarragon

**Serves 4**

### FOR THE HERBED COUSCOUS
175g (6oz) couscous
3 tbsp olive oil
Juice of ½ a lemon or orange
300ml (10fl oz) water
A pinch (¼ level tsp) freshly ground black pepper
2 level tbsp chopped fresh herbs, such as
   coriander, flat parsley or mint

### FOR THE CHICKEN
4 chicken breasts, skin removed
   (preferably free-range or organic chicken)
10g (½ oz) butter, softened but not melted
300g (10½ oz) leeks, trimmed and sliced
4 tbsp cream
2 level tsp fresh tarragon, chopped
A pinch (¼ level tsp) freshly ground black pepper

Preheat the oven to 170°C/300°F/Gas 3. Place the couscous in a heatproof bowl. Add 2 tablespoons of olive oil and the lemon juice and mix gently but thoroughly. Heat the water to a simmer and pour it over the couscous. Allow the couscous to absorb the liquid, stirring occasionally with a fork to encourage the grains to separate. This will take about 20 minutes. Cover the bowl with tinfoil and place in the oven for about 15 minutes for the couscous to warm through.

While the couscous is cooking, place a small frying pan on a low heat to gently warm up. The pan should be just big enough to hold the chicken. The pan should be moderately hot before the chicken is added. Smear the softened butter over the surface of the chicken breasts. Place buttered side down in the pan and cook on a gentle heat to turn a golden brown colour. Turn and repeat on the other side. Season with a little black pepper. Cover the pan with greaseproof paper or a butter wrapper and a tight fitting lid. This is crucial, so, if you don't have a lid that fits the pan tightly, use a plate or some such. Do not have the heat too low or the chicken will not brown and if the heat is too high the butter will burn and the sauce will be spoiled later.

After 10 minutes, check to see if the chicken is nearly cooked. The breasts should feel quite firm to the touch. Briefly remove the chicken to a plate. Add the sliced leeks to the pan and toss in the buttery chicken juices. Place the chicken back in the pan. Cover tightly again as before and cook for a further 6–7 minutes until the leeks are tender and the chicken is cooked through.

Remove the lid, add the cream and tarragon and place on a low heat to allow the cream to bubble up just once. The cream will thicken slightly and that is your sauce, scant yes, but surely delicious.

Serve immediately with herbed couscous.

* Please note the garnish in the photograph was included for illustration purposes only.

 *If possible, buy organic chicken and leeks. You will be rewarded by the superior taste and texture. The trick here is to keep the pan really tightly covered while the chicken and leeks are cooking, as this prevents the cooking juices from the chicken evaporating in the form of steam. Cooking the chicken and leeks on a gentle heat is also important, as no liquid is added to the pan until the end of cooking. There is a very small amount of sauce, but it should be highly flavoured.*

 ***Per portion*** *this dish provides 1½ portions of vegetables and 4½ protein exchanges.*

*Check your daily allowances to see if you have enough remaining for this dish.*

# Roast Peaches or Nectarines with Honey

**Serves 4**

4 peaches or nectarines, 440g (15oz)
1½ tbsp runny honey
1½ tbsp lemon juice
25g (1oz) butter
125g (4oz) natural yoghurt, to serve

Preheat the oven to 220°C/425°F/Gas 7.

Halve the fruit and remove the stones. Place them in a snugly fitting ovenproof dish. Melt the butter and add the honey and lemon. Spoon the mixture over the fruit, place in the oven and cook for 8–10 minutes or until the fruit is tender but still holding its shape.

Serve in wide-rimmed bowls with a blob of natural yoghurt.

***Per portion*** *this dessert provides 1 portion of fruit.*

*If you have a daily allowance of dairy products please note that there is yoghurt in this recipe, which needs to be taken from your allowance.*

*Check your daily allowances to see if you have enough remaining for this dessert.*

\* Please note the garnish in the photograph was included for illustration purposes only.

# Ross Lewis

## *All Good Cooking Starts with Good Shopping*

After studying dairy science at University College Cork, Ross Lewis did what a lot of other graduates did in the 1980s. "I headed off to America on a J1 visa and ended up working in a restaurant in New York. I decided there and then this was the life for me."

Returning home from America, Ross worked in London and then decided he wanted to open his own restaurant. "My mother's family came from an agricultural background – they always had their own milk and grew their own vegetables. When we moved to Bishopstown in Cork city, my mother continued to grow vegetables in our garden and she always had great food prepared for the family. Growing up with this, my family soon found that there were only two things I was interested in. One was hammering nails into wood and the other was cooking. So I was either going to be a carpenter or a chef!"

It was February 1992 when Ross opened Chapter One in the basement of the Dublin Writers' Museum in Parnell Square. "We are here now seventeen years and in that time I have seen some of the food producers in Ireland come on in leaps and bounds. We have fantastic artisan food producers in this country but I am disappointed with the way we handle fish in Ireland. We have some of the best fish in the world and, instead of using this wonderful product here, we send it by the truckload to France and Spain."

At home, Ross loves to spend time teaching his three daughters about good food. "We like to get the children involved when I cook at home. It all starts with shopping together and we go to the Dún Laoghaire farmers' market every week. At home, it's really simple stuff like pot-roast chicken and really good soups. I try to show the girls that you can't have good cooking without good shopping: that's where it all begins."

For Ross, that is the essence of good cooking. "If you start with the best ingredients, then you can't go far wrong. Really good ingredients don't need much done to them; food is at its best when its true flavour is allowed to speak for itself. Simplicity – that's the best way to go."

As for Ross's recipes in this book: "Just enjoy – that's what cooking and working with food is all about. Try different things – don't be afraid of it. Remember, food can be a lot more than just fuel for your body. Get involved in every aspect of it. If you can, try to grow some of your own vegetables but also remember a good meal starts with good shopping, so talk to your butcher and grocer and find out where your food is coming from. This will make every meal special – and the food you cook for your family and friends more rewarding."

*Chapter One, 18–19 Parnell Square, Dublin 1. Tel: 01 8732266; www.chapteronerestaurant.com*

# Melon and Raspberries with Cinnamon Jelly and Fresh Basil

**Serves 6**

470g (1lb) Honeydew melon flesh
120g (4oz) fresh raspberries
6 fresh basil leaves, chopped finely, to serve
A pinch (¼ level tsp) freshly grated nutmeg, to serve

**FOR THE APPLE AND CINNAMON JELLY**
200ml (7fl oz) apple juice
150ml (5fl oz) water
225g (8oz) caster sugar
A squeeze of fresh lemon juice
A pinch (¼ level tsp) ground cinnamon
3 gelatine leaves

To make the jelly, bring all the ingredients except the gelatine to the boil in a pan and simmer for 5 minutes. Soften the gelatine in a little water in a glass and, when soft, squeeze out and add to mix. Strain into a large, shallow dish or baking tray, then cover well and refrigerate for 12 hours. Then turn the jelly out on to a large chopping board and cut into small cubes. (Alternatively you could make the jelly in ice-cube trays and then cut the cubes of jelly in half to serve.)

Ahead of serving, scoop the melon into balls, using a melon baller, then scrape all of the remaining flesh into a juicer or food processor and purée it.

Divide the melon purée between suitable plates or bowls and arrange the melon balls and raspberries on top.

To serve, arrange cubes of apple and cinnamon jelly around the dish and decorate with finely sliced basil and a little freshly grated nutmeg.

 **Per portion** this dish provides 1½ portions of fruit.

*Check your daily allowances to see if you have enough remaining for this dish.*

# Turbot, Red Pepper Escabeche, Virgin Olive Oil and Basil

**Serves 4**

**FOR THE RED PEPPER ESCABECHE**

350g (12oz) red pepper,
   halved and seeded
40g (1½oz) shallots, diced
1 garlic clove, crushed
50ml (2fl oz) olive oil
½ level tsp dried chilli powder
130g (4½oz) plum tomatoes, skinned,
   seeded and sliced
1 level tsp fresh thyme, chopped
1 level tsp fresh basil, chopped
1 tbsp red wine vinegar

**FOR THE TURBOT**

4 turbot fillets (approx. 175g/6oz each)
2 tbsp olive oil
2 tsp (10ml) freshly squeezed lemon juice,
   plus extra to serve
1 garlic clove, crushed
2 level tsp of any soft green herb such as
   parsley, chives or dill, roughly chopped

2 fresh basil leaves per portion, to garnish

To roast the peppers, preheat the oven to 200°/400°/Gas 6. Coat the peppers in a little olive oil and then roast in an ovenproof dish for 15 minutes or until the skin is blistered but not burnt. Then let the peppers cool, peel them and chop them into chunks. Set aside.

To make the red pepper escabeche, sweat the shallots and garlic in olive oil and add the chilli powder. Add the roasted red pepper and all the other ingredients. Cover and cook over a low heat for about 5 minutes, stirring occasionally. Then remove the lid and cook for a further 10 minutes. Then remove from the heat. Strain the mixture through a sieve to remove any lumps and then pour the strained liquid back into the pan and cook for a further 5 minutes to thicken the sauce and intensify the flavour.

Meanwhile, reduce the oven temperature to 180°C/350°F/Gas 4. Place each turbot fillet on a square of tinfoil, big enough to fold into a parcel around the fish. Sprinkle ½ tbsp of olive oil over each fillet, then add some freshly squeezed lemon juice, a little crushed garlic and a little of the soft green herbs such as parsley, chives or dill. Fold up the tinfoil to enclose the fish and bake the parcels for about 10 minutes, until the fish is cooked through and the flesh is pearly white. You may then brown the fish under a hot grill.

* Please note the garnish of the globe artichoke in the photograph was included for illustration purposes only.

To serve, place each fillet on a warmed plate with some red pepper sauce on the side. Season each fillet with a squeeze of lemon juice and garnish with fresh basil leaves.

This dish can be served with freshly cooked rice.

 **Per portion** *this dish provides 1½ portions of vegetables and 4½ protein exchanges.*

*Check your daily allowances to see if you have enough remaining for this dish.*

# Lemon Crème Caramel with Mango Purée

**Serves 6**

**FOR THE CRÈME CARAMEL**
300ml (10fl oz) milk
Zest of 1 lemon
2 eggs plus 1 egg yolk
75g (3oz) sugar

**FOR THE CARAMEL**
100g (3½oz) sugar

**FOR THE MANGO PURÉE**
300g (10½oz) mangoes, peeled, stoned and roughly chopped
Juice of 1 lime
A pinch (¼ level tsp) caster sugar

**FOR THE MANGO SALAD**
150g (5oz) mango, peeled and stoned
6 fresh mint leaves

6 x 100ml (3½fl oz) dariole moulds

To make the crème caramel, blend the crème caramel ingredients in a liquidiser, then place the mixture in a bowl. Cover with clingfilm, place in the fridge and leave to chill overnight. The next day pass the mixture through a sieve.

To make the caramel, heat the sugar in a pan over a low heat, without stirring. When it turns dark in colour, pour a little of the mixture into the bottom of each of your dariole moulds and allow to set.

Preheat the oven to 170°C/325°F/Gas 3.

When the caramel is set, pour the crème caramel mixture on top. Then place the dariole moulds into a large roasting tin and half-fill the tin with boiling water until the water level reaches halfway up the side of the dariole moulds. Cook the crème caramel in this bain marie for 1 hour in the oven. Remove from oven and allow to cool.

While the crème caramel is cooking, make the mango purée and mango salad. To make the mango purée, liquidise the mangoes, lime juice and sugar and then pass through a sieve. To make the mango salad, slice the mango very thinly, finely chop the mint leaves and mix together gently.

To serve, dot the mango purée around the plate. To de-mould each crème caramel, dip the mould briefly in hot water and then tip it out gently onto the plate. Place a little mango salad beside the crème caramel.

 ***Per portion*** *this dessert provides 1 portion of fruit and ½ a protein exchange.*

*While you don't usually think of desserts as having a lot of protein, this recipe has the equivalent of about ½ an egg per portion and therefore it has been counted in the protein allowances for this recipe. If you have a daily allowance of dairy products, please note that there is milk in this recipe, which needs to be taken from your allowance.*

*Check your daily allowances to see if you have enough remaining for this dessert.*

Vegetarian
Chefs

Irish Nutrition and Dietetic Institute

A word from the

# RENAL DIETITIANS

## A GUIDE TO USING THE VEGETARIAN SECTION

To make this book as useful as possible a vegetarian section was proposed. Recipes in this section are suitable for vegetarians, lacto-ovo and ovo vegetarians. Recipes are not suitable for vegans.

Vegetarianism and the renal diet represent a major challenge to us as dietitians as many staple foods in the vegetarian diet, for example peas, beans and lentils, are not generally included due to the high levels of potassium and phosphate in these foods.

Avoidance of animal-based foods (for example, meat and fish) means that other dietary sources of protein must be used to meet protein requirements for the different stages of kidney disease. It can be difficult to achieve your optimal protein intake whilst ensuring that potassium and phosphate levels are well controlled.

The recipes in this section, thanks to the creativity of the chefs, have ensured tasty recipes that can be included in the renal diet. Coding at the end of each recipe is based largely on the renal diet sheet that your dietitian has/will discuss with you.

### PROTEIN

Each recipe has been coded with the number of protein exchanges it provides per portion. Protein sources in recipes include tofu and pulses (including beans, lentils and chickpeas). If you are a lacto-ovo vegetarian, eggs are used in some recipes, which are a good source of protein.

### DAIRY PRODUCTS AND PHOSPHATE

Dairy products not only provide us with protein but also potassium and phosphate. Recipes containing dairy products have been coded to tell you the number of dairy exchanges they contain per portion. 1 dairy exchange is equal to 200ml of milk or 1oz cheese or 125g yoghurt. Note soya based dairy products can be used in recipes to replace milk, cheese or yoghurt; however, these foods must still be counted as part of your dairy food exchanges. If you have been prescribed phosphate binders, it is important to take them with your meals.

## SALT

As most adults with kidney disease require a salt restricted diet, all the recipes in this section are low in salt. You will notice in many of the recipes that tinned pulses have been used. It is important to remember that when you are using tinned pulses, to purchase "no added salt varieties". Other varieties of tinned pulses should be avoided as they are too high in salt.

## POTASSIUM

Potassium is found in many foods, but is most concentrated in fruit, vegetables and juices. All these foods are staples within a vegetarian diet. With kidney failure, the amount of potassium in the body can rise too high. This is dangerous as it can cause a heart attack.

If you are on a potassium restriction, you will need to restrict your fruit, vegetable and potato intake. In addition, potatoes must be boiled (as per page 282) to reduce the potassium content. You will also need to avoid foods that are high in potassium (check your diet sheet or talk to your dietitian).

Each of the recipes in this section have been coded to tell you how many portions of fruit or vegetables that they contain. **Please check with your dietitian, what your daily allowance is, for each of these foods.**

## HOW CAN I USE THESE RECIPES IF I AM NOT A VEGETARIAN?

Finally, some of the recipes in this section may appeal to you even if you are not vegetarian. However, you should discuss with you dietitian how to include recipes safely into your meal plan and daily allowances.

Denis Cotter

# Denis Cotter

## *Eat as Many Good Things as You Possibly Can*

After spending years working in a bank, Denis Cotter decided he needed a change. "When I was with the bank, I did a lot of travelling, doing internal audits and so on. Because of the travelling, I found myself eating out a lot, and one day I realised I was more interested in the eating than the auditing. I became obsessed with restaurants and food."

So, taking a year's leave of absence from the bank, Denis headed for London and never looked back. In London he took a job at the famous Cranks Restaurant. "I started out clearing tables and working at the counter, then one day I ended up in the kitchen – and so began my informal training."

Denis decided to travel again and took off for New Zealand. It was there that he learned about the importance of fresh, local and seasonal ingredients. "When we started our vegetarian restaurant, Café Paradiso in Cork, we wanted our food to have the best organic ingredients available, no matter where they came from. Now, fifteen years later, our focus is still on the produce. One of our star producers is Ultan Walsh, who supplies us from his farm outside Cork. Working with local food and local producers is top of our list."

Denis will visit the farm once every couple of weeks to get inspiration for his menu at the restaurant and to see what he has to look forward to in the weeks ahead. "Ultan is always trying to grow new vegetables for us to serve here in the restaurant. That is what seasonal cooking is all about: getting the best out of food at its freshest."

At home, Denis likes to continue the seasonal food ethic when it comes to his cooking. "I don't really have one favourite food. For me, it's all about what's good right now. I like food that is balanced – sweet and spicy, for example. Balance comes from variety, so you should eat as many good things as you can."

Denis is often asked if it is easier to cook vegetables or meat. "I think, if anything, it is harder to cook vegetables well. With meat, you can fry, grill or roast – with vegetables, you have to construct different complex flavours."

For the renal cookbook, Denis found the list of ingredients a bit of a challenge. "When I first received the list, I thought it was going to be easy but the more I got into the process, I found that the ingredients I would instinctively reach for could not be used. The whole project really made me focus more on how to get the best flavours from the foods we could include.

"It was a very interesting challenge; I had to think twice about everything. For people who will be making my recipes, I would say that, of course, buy the best possible ingredients from what is allowed. But, remember, the whole process should be a pleasurable one – not just the cooking or even the eating of the food; the selection of the raw ingredients is also a part of the event."

*Café Paradiso, 16 Lancaster Quay, Cork city. Tel: 021 4277939; www.cafeparadiso.ie*

# Roast Pepper Hummus

**Serves 6, as a starter or party dip**

1 red pepper
400g (14oz) can of cooked chickpeas, drained and rinsed (approx. 230g/8oz)
2 level tbsp tahini (sesame seed paste)
2 garlic cloves, crushed
1 level tsp cumin seeds, ground
½ level tsp paprika
Juice of 1 lemon
2 tbsp olive oil

Lightly toasted pitta bread, water biscuits, toasted bagel or baguette, to serve

Roast the pepper in a hot oven (200°C/400°F/Gas 6), over a flame or under a grill, until the skin is blackened all over. Place the pepper in a bowl, cover tightly with clingfilm and leave to cool. Once cooled the pepper will be easy to peel as the skin will have lifted. Remove the skin and seeds.

Coarsely chop the pepper flesh and put it in a food processor with the chickpeas, tahini, garlic and spices. Blend to a fine purée. Add lemon juice to taste. With the motor running, add some or all of the oil as you go, to get a smooth, light texture.

Spoon into a bowl set on a plate and serve with lightly toasted pitta bread, water biscuits, toasted bagel or baguette.

 *Per portion* this dish provides ½ a portion of vegetables and ½ a protein exchange.

*Check your daily allowances to see if you have enough remaining for this dish.*

# Grilled Courgette, Green Bean and Lentil Salad with Coriander, Mint and Yoghurt Dressing

**Serves 6**

200g (7oz) dried puy lentils
600ml (1 pint) water
200g (7oz) courgettes, halved lengthways
100ml (3½fl oz) olive oil
400g (14oz) green beans, trimmed
1 medium red onion, halved and thinly sliced

1 level tsp ground cumin
2 level tbsp fresh coriander, chopped
1 level tbsp fresh mint, chopped
Juice of 1 lemon
100ml (3½fl oz) yoghurt

Rinse the lentils in a sieve under cold running water, then place them in a pan with 600ml (1 pint) of water. Bring to the boil, then reduce the heat and let simmer for 15–20 minutes or until they are al dente. Drain in a sieve and set aside.

Brush the courgettes with a little of the olive oil and cook them under a hot grill or in a hot oven at 200°C/400°F/Gas 6 until lightly coloured.

Cook the green beans in a pot of boiling water for 5–6 minutes, until just done. Drain and cool briefly in cold water.

Put the vegetables in a large bowl with the cooked lentils, cumin and herbs. Combine the lemon juice and yoghurt with the rest of the olive oil and fold into the salad, keeping some dressing aside.

Serve the salad in shallow bowls with a little more of the dressing drizzled over and around each portion.

 ***Per portion*** *this dish provides 2 portions of vegetables and ½ a protein exchange.*

*If you have a daily allowance of dairy products, please note that there is yoghurt in this recipe, which needs to be taken from your allowance.*

*Check your daily allowances to see if you have enough remaining for this dish.*

# Honey-Glazed Tofu with Rice Noodles and Greens in Ginger Coconut Sauce

**Serves 4**

(LF)

### FOR THE HONEY-GLAZED TOFU

3 tbsp honey

1 tbsp white wine vinegar

1 level tsp dried chilli powder

2 tbsp water

500g (18oz) tofu, in 16 slices

2 tbsp vegetable oil

### FOR THE NOODLES

160g (5½oz) wide rice noodles

1 lime

### FOR THE GREENS IN GINGER COCONUT SAUCE

1 medium white onion (approx. 100g), halved and thinly sliced

200g (7oz) green cabbage, core removed and thinly sliced

30g (1¼oz) fresh ginger, peeled and grated

1 level tsp coriander seeds, coarsely chopped

80ml (3fl oz) coconut milk

80ml (3fl oz) water

To prepare the tofu, combine the honey, vinegar, chilli and 2 tablespoons of water to make a marinade. Add the tofu and leave for 15–30 minutes to allow the flavours to penetrate.

Heat a wok or large frying pan and brush it with vegetable oil. Put in some of the tofu and fry over medium heat for 2 minutes on each side, until browned. Add some of the marinade and continue cooking until it has been absorbed. Repeat until all the tofu is cooked. Set aside or keep warm in a low oven.

Heat some more oil in the pan and fry the vegetables for 5–8 minutes, to your liking. Add the ginger, coriander seeds, and then coconut milk and water. Bring to a boil and simmer for 3–4 minutes.

At the same time, bring a pot of water to a boil and cook the noodles according to the packet instructions. This usually means simmering over a very low heat for 8–10 minutes and draining in a colander.

Place some rice noodles in each of your four bowls with some vegetables on top, pouring the coconut broth in too. Arrange the tofu on top and squeeze some lime juice over each portion to serve.

 **Per portion** *this dish provides 1½ portions of vegetables and 1½ protein exchanges.*

*Check your daily allowances to see if you have enough remaining for this dish.*

Denis Cotter

# Pumpkin, Red Onion and Cheddar Cheese Tortilla with Roast Garlic Aïoli

**Serves 6**

| FOR THE AÏOLI | FOR THE PUMPKIN TORTILLA |
|---|---|
| 1 garlic bulb, 40g (1½oz) | 300g (10½oz) pumpkin flesh (seeded and cut into dices) |
| 1 egg | 2 red onions, thinly sliced |
| 1 egg yolk | 2 tbsp olive oil |
| 1 level tsp prepared mustard | 10 eggs |
| 200ml (7fl oz) olive oil | 1 handful fresh basil leaves (approx. 15g), coarsely chopped |
| Juice of 1 lemon, to taste | 15g (½oz) Cheddar cheese made with pasteurised milk, diced |

Preheat the oven to 180°C/350°F/Gas 4. Cut the end off the garlic bulb. Toss the bulb lightly in a little of the olive oil and place it on a small oven dish in the hot oven for 15–20 minutes, until the garlic bulb is soft and lightly coloured. Squeeze the flesh from the skin and put it in a food processor. Add the eggs and mustard and blend for 2 minutes. Slowly add the oil until the aïoli has the consistency you want. Add lemon juice to taste.

Toss the pumpkin and red onion in half the olive oil in an ovenproof dish, and roast in the oven for 20–30 minutes, until tender and lightly browned. Meanwhile, in a large bowl, beat the eggs and stir in the cooked pumpkin and onion mixture with the basil and Cheddar.

Preheat the grill. Place a large heavy pan over a low heat and brush it with the remaining olive oil. Pour in the egg mixture, patting it down quickly and briefly. Leave it to cook for 7 minutes. Check that the base is cooked by lifting the edges with a spatula. Place the pan under a low grill to set the top a little without browning it. Loosen the tortilla with a spatula or slice, and slide it on to a large plate. Place the pan over the plate and flip the plate over quickly to put the tortilla back in the pan top-side down. Tuck in the edges and put the pan back on the low heat for a further 5–7 minutes. Turn off the heat and leave the tortilla for another 5 minutes at least. Slide it on to a clean plate.

To serve, cut the tortilla into wedges and serve each with a dollop of aïoli on the plate.

 **Per portion** this dish provides 1½ portions of vegetables and 2 protein exchanges.

*If you have a daily allowance of dairy products, please note that there is cheese in this recipe, which needs to be taken from your allowance.*

*Check your daily allowances to see that you have enough remaining for this dish.*

227

# Blackcurrant Fool with Orange Sponge Fingers

**Serves 6**

500g (18oz) blackcurrants, fresh or frozen
300g (11oz) sugar
1 tbsp water
300ml (10fl oz) cream
2 eggs, separated

50g (2oz) caster sugar
50g (2oz) plain flour
20g (¾oz) cornflour
Zest of 1 orange
Icing sugar, to serve

Put the fruit in a pan with the sugar and water. Bring it very slowly to the boil and simmer gently, stirring occasionally, until the fruit is very soft. Blend the fruit in a food processor, pass the purée through a sieve and leave to cool.

Whisk the cream to soft peaks and then fold in the purée. Save a little of the purée to swirl on the top of individual portions. You can serve the fool now or chill it again for up to a few hours before serving.

To make the sponge fingers, preheat the oven to 180°C/350°F/Gas 4. Whisk the egg whites until stiff, then add half the caster sugar and whisk again for a minute. In another bowl, whisk the egg yolks and the rest of the caster sugar until pale and fluffy. Sift the flour and cornflour together and fold into the beaten egg yolks. Then fold the egg whites into the flour and egg yolk mixture. Mix in the orange zest.

Use a piping bag to pipe lengths of the batter, 10 x 2cm (4 x 1in), on to baking trays lined with parchment.

Bake for 25–30 minutes, until pale golden. Leave to cool on the trays. Dredge the fingers with icing sugar before serving. To serve set the fingers on a plate with the blackcurrant fool.

 *This recipe can be adapted to use blackberries or gooseberries instead.*

 **Per portion** *this dessert provides 2 portions of fruit.*

*If blackberries or gooseberries are used in place of blackcurrants in this recipe, the recipe provides only 1 portion of fruit.*

*Check your daily allowances to see if you have enough remaining for this dessert.*

# Pear, Pomegranate and Maple Tarte Tatin

**Serves 6**

50g (2oz) butter
30g (1oz) caster sugar
3 tbsp maple syrup
2 tbsp pomegranate juice
6 medium-sized firm pears, peeled, quartered and cored
½ level tsp ground cinnamon
A pinch (¼ level tsp) grated nutmeg
1 x 250g (9oz) sheet of all-butter puff pastry
180ml (6½fl oz) cream, to serve

Preheat the oven to 200°C/400°F/Gas 6.

Place an ovenproof frying pan over a medium heat on the stove and melt the butter. Add in the caster sugar, maple syrup and pomegranate juice and stir gently until the mixture begins to caramelise. Add the pears and the spice and stir well to coat the pears in the liquid. Continue cooking the pears, stirring occasionally, for 10 minutes or until the syrup has thickened.

Push the pears with a spatula to make sure they are packed towards the centre of the pan.

Roll out the pastry and place it over the top of the pears. Cut off any excess pastry, leaving 2–3cm (¾–1¼in) all round. Use a spatula to push this excess into the pan and around the pears. Prick the pastry with a fork. Place the ovenproof frying pan on an oven tray and put this in the oven. Bake for 20–30 minutes, until the pastry is browned and crisp.

Remove the dish from the oven and leave to stand for 10 minutes. Place a plate on top and carefully flip the pan over to invert the tarte on to the plate. If any pears get stuck, free them with a spatula and press them back on to the tarte.

Slice and serve with lightly whipped cream.

 **Per portion** this dessert provides 1½ portions of fruit.

*Check your daily allowances to see if you have enough remaining for this dessert.*

Lorraine Fitzmaurice

## You Are What You Eat

Healthy eating has always been a fact of life for Lorraine Fitzmaurice. Unlike most children, Lorraine was raised eating a macrobiotic diet. "My parents brought us up on a macrobiotic diet. There were four kids running around at home and we spent most of our time in the kitchen with my mother. I can remember that at the age of about ten, I would make the Sunday dinner every week – so I suppose you might say that I have always been cooking."

Lorraine's parents opened the first wholefood restaurant in Dublin in 1977. "During the summer holidays and at the weekends, we would hang around the restaurant and I really learned a lot about food and cooking there. I didn't go to a cookery school or college. I just seemed to pick it all up from my parents at the restaurant."

What was it like for a child in Ireland growing up on a macrobiotic diet? "We didn't know any other way. As kids, we didn't know that we ate any differently to our friends, but when our friends would come to our house, for a birthday party or something, that's when we realised that people were eating different food to us. Again, when I went to secondary school and people would look in my lunch box, the reaction was sometimes, 'Oh my God, what are you eating?' But we never thought about our diet – it was simply the way we ate, full stop."

Today, Lorraine is glad that her diet was different to everybody else's. "Now I find that I have more energy than a lot of people my age. I am a great believer in the old saying 'you are what you eat'. Good food equals a healthy body."

Lorraine describes her cooking style as simple home cooking with an emphasis on healthy, fresh food. "My style is just the style that I grew up with. This is how I eat; this is what comes naturally to me. For example, my diet is very grain-based, and I like to have tofu or beans as a side dish. I do like fish but, unlike most typical Irish families, we would have potatoes only once or twice a month."

For Lorraine, it is not only the cooking of good food that gives her so much pleasure. "I love sitting down and sharing a good meal with friends and family. I think that you should make your meals an event, no matter how simple your meal is. Cooking for me is healing; it can restore your energy.

"For my recipes in this book, I would like people to try something new every day for a month. Good food can help make you feel better; it makes a difference to your body and mind. I really believe this philosophy and would like to see people putting more effort into their diets. You will feel the difference."

*The Blazing Salads Food Company, 42 Drury Street, Dublin 2.*
*Tel: 01 6718612; www.blazingsalads.com*

# Wholemeal Loaf

**Makes one large loaf (approx. 15 slices)**

15g (½oz) fresh yeast
350ml (12fl oz) tepid water
210g (7¼oz) white flour

320g (11oz) organic wholemeal flour
1 level tsp natural sea salt
Sunflower oil, for brushing

Blend the fresh yeast with about 100ml (3½fl oz) of the water and set aside for a couple of minutes.

Mix the flours and salt together, make a well in the centre and pour in the yeast mixture with the rest of the water. Knead the dough for 10 minutes. Kneading is essentially stretching and folding the dough to develop the gluten in it. The most common technique is using one hand to hold the dough in place while you stretch the dough away from you by pushing it with the heel of the palm of your other hand. The stretched end is then folded back towards you. Then turn the dough a quarter turn and repeat as before. The dough will become smooth and elastic in the process

Place the dough in a large, clean mixing bowl, cover and leave to prove somewhere warm for 1 hour or until the dough has doubled in size.

Preheat the oven to 200°C/400°F/Gas 6. Uncover the dough, turn out on to a clean work surface and gently knock the air out of it. This is done by turning the dough out on a clean surface, gently pinching it and squashing the air out of the dough with your knuckles. It is necessary to get all the air out at this stage. Then fold the dough into a smooth oblong shape, pinching the seam together. Set aside, seam-side down, and cover with a damp tea towel for 15 minutes.

Uncover the dough, place it, seam side down, in a lightly oiled 900g (2lb) baking tin and lightly spray with water. With the palm of your hand, press down firmly on the dough, forcing it into the shape of the tin. Cover and set aside at room temperature for 30 minutes, until it rises to just above the rim of the tin. Using the indentation test, check whether the dough is ready to be baked. Press your finger about 1cm (½in) into the dough and, if it only springs back halfway, it's ready.

Spray the oven with water 5 minutes before putting the loaf in. Uncover and cut an incision along the top of the dough lengthwise to about 1cm (½in) deep. Place the loaf in the centre of the oven and spray again with water. Lower the temperature to 180°C/350°F/Gas 4 and bake for 45–60 minutes until cooked through and lightly golden brown on top. After 5 minutes transfer to a wire rack and leave to cool completely before cutting into slices to serve.

 *This bread is higher in phosphate and potassium than white bread, therefore if you are on a phosphate or potassium restriction you need to discuss this recipe with your dietitian.*

# Wholemeal Scones

**Makes 20 scones**

1kg (2¼lb) thick natural yoghurt
1 tsp honey
2 level tbsp baking soda
650g (1lb 6oz) organic strong wholemeal
    flour, plus extra for dusting

650g (1lb 6oz) white flour
½ level tsp natural sea salt
3 level tbsp sunflower margarine
Milk, for brushing

Preheat the oven to 190°C/375°F/Gas 5.

Place the yoghurt in a large bowl. Beat in the honey and baking soda. Set aside to rise. Place the flour, salt and margarine in a large bowl. Rub in the margarine with your fingertips. Pour in the yoghurt mixture and stir, making sure all the dry flour is mixed well in.

Turn out on to a floured surface and knead gently until a soft dough forms. It is important to think light and to use light hands to ensure that the scones will be light. Press out until the dough is 1cm (½in) deep. Using a small scone cutter, cut out the scones. Keep bringing the leftover dough mixture together until all the dough has been used up. It should make about 20 scones. Place them on a lightly floured baking sheet and brush with milk.

Bake on the centre shelf of the oven for 30–40 minutes or until the scones have risen and are golden in colour.

 *Each scone contains ½ a dairy exchange.*

*These scones are higher in phosphate and potassium than white bread therefore if you are on a phosphate or potassium restriction you need to discuss this recipe with your dietitian.*

*Check your daily allowances to see if you have enough remaining for this scone.*

# Vegetable and Tofu Spring Rolls with Sweet Chilli Sauce

**Makes 10 rolls**

**FOR THE SPRING ROLL FILLING**

2 medium onions, peeled
3 medium carrots, peeled
200g (7oz) courgettes, trimmed
1 tbsp unrefined sunflower oil
A pinch (¼ level tsp) natural sea salt
3 x 160g (5½oz) cubes of tofu
1 tbsp water
A pinch (¼ level tsp) freshly ground pepper

**FOR THE SWEET CHILLI SAUCE**

2–3 spring onions
1 tbsp light sesame oil
1 level tsp fresh ginger, peeled and finely grated
15g (½oz) red chilli, seeded and finely chopped
2 tbsp fresh lemon juice
2 tbsp clear honey

**FOR MAKING THE SPRING ROLLS**

1 packet (230g) spring roll pastry, 20 sheets of 21 x 21cm (9x9in)
2 level tsp cornflour
55ml (2fl oz) water
Natural sunflower oil, for deep-frying

To prepare the spring roll filling, slice the onions into thin half-moon pieces. Slice the carrots first in half lengthwise, then slice into thin diagonal pieces. Slice the courgettes in half lengthwise, then slice into thin diagonal pieces. Sauté the onions in a little unrefined sunflower oil for 3 minutes. Add the carrots and courgettes and the salt. Add the tablespoon of water, cover with a lid and cook the vegetables until tender but not mushy. Crumble the tofu into large pieces and stir into the vegetables. Season with pepper. Don't season too much as the spring rolls are accompanied by a dipping sauce. Allow to cool.

To make the dip, in a small pan sauté the spring onions in sesame oil over a medium heat for 1 minute. Add the ginger, red chilli, lemon juice and honey. Simmer for another minute and place into small bowls as a dip.

To prepare the spring rolls, separate the pastry, allowing 2 sheets per spring roll. Divide the filling into 10 portions. Place 2 sheets of pastry on top of each other in a diamond shape in front of you. Place one of the filling portions on the pastry about 2.5cm (1in) from the bottom point. Roll up firmly, folding in the sides when you reach halfway. Roll to 2.5cm

(1in) of pastry at the top. Blend the cornflour mix in a small bowl. Brush the pastry generously with the cornflour and water mix and use to seal up the spring rolls.

When all the rolls are ready, heat the natural sunflower oil in a wok or large pan for deep-frying. Never leave the pan of hot oil unattended. To check the oil is hot enough, drop a crust of bread into the oil and it should come up to the surface immediately. Once the oil has come up to temperature, fry 3 spring rolls at a time, for about 5 minutes, until crisp and golden. They will fry better if done in batches. Once cooked, leave to sit on a paper towel.

Serve the spring rolls immediately on plates with bowls of the sweet chilli dipping sauce.

 *Each spring roll provides 1½ portions of vegetables and ½ a protein exchange.*

*Check your daily allowances to see if you have enough remaining for this dish.*

# Tofu Chilli

**Serves 4**

1 tbsp sunflower oil
½ medium onion (approx. 95g/3½oz), finely diced
1 garlic clove, minced
15g (½oz) red chilli, seeded and minced
½ green pepper, seeded and finely diced
½ yellow pepper, seeded and finely diced
1 x 400g (14oz) can plum tomatoes, drained weight = 240g
A pinch (¼ level tsp) sea salt
320g (12oz) tofu, crumbled
150g (5oz) canned red kidney beans, drained and rinsed
1 level tbsp fresh coriander, chopped
200ml (7fl oz) water
A pinch (¼ level tsp) coarsely ground black pepper

Basmati rice, to serve.

Add the sunflower oil to a hot pan and sauté the onion until soft. Add the garlic, chilli and peppers and sauté for a further 3 minutes.

Drain the tinned tomatoes and chop them, discarding the juices. Add to the pot with the salt. Bring to the boil and then lower the heat and simmer on a low heat for 30 minutes, stirring occasionally.

Add the tofu to the pot along with the kidney beans and fresh coriander. Add the water and allow to simmer for 5 minutes. Season with pepper.

Serve in wide-rimmed, deep bowls with basmati rice on the side.

 ***Per portion*** *this dish provides 2 portions of vegetables and 1½ protein exchanges. Check your daily allowances to see if you have enough remaining for this dish.*

Lorraine Fitzmaurice

# Carrot Cake

**Serves 20**

115ml (4fl oz) sunflower oil
4 free-range eggs
60ml (2½fl oz) soya milk or cow's milk
75g (3oz) sunflower margarine
120ml (4fl oz) honey
265g (10oz) carrot, grated
200g (7oz) fine wholemeal flour
70g (2½oz) white flour
15g (½oz) bread soda
Zest of 1 large orange
¾ level tsp ground cinnamon

**FOR THE TOPPING**

250g (9oz) cream cheese made with
    pasteurised milk
Zest of ½ orange
1 tbsp milk
1 tbsp maple syrup or honey

Preheat the oven to 190°C/375°F/Gas 5. Oil and line the base of a 23cm (9in) baking tin with parchment paper.

In a large bowl whisk the eggs until light and fluffy. Add the milk, oil, margarine and honey and whisk until smooth. Stir the grated carrot into the mixture.

In a separate bowl, mix the flours, bread soda, orange zest and cinnamon together. Add to the wet egg mixture and mix well, making sure all the dry ingredients have been mixed in. Pour into your oiled and base-lined baking tin. Bake in the oven on the centre shelf for 1 hour until the cake is springy to the touch. Set aside to cool thoroughly.

To make the topping, combine all the topping ingredients in a bowl and mix until smooth.

When the cake is completely cooled, remove from the tin and spread topping over the cake generously. Cut into slices to serve.

*This carrot cake freezes very well, but freeze it without the topping. When ready to use, defrost the cake thoroughly and then put the topping on.*

*Each slice of cake provides ½ a portion of vegetables.*

*Check your daily allowances to see if you have enough remaining for this cake.*

Deirdre McCafferty
& Tony Keogh

# Deirdre McCafferty & Tony Keogh

## *A Winning Team*

Mention Cornucopia in Dublin and people will smile when they tell you about the good food they've enjoyed in this landmark vegetarian restaurant on Wicklow Street. For Deirdre McCafferty and chef Tony Keogh, Cornucopia is not just a restaurant: it's a way of life.

Deirdre and her late husband, Neil, set up the vegetarian restaurant when they returned to Dublin in 1986. "Having worked and studied in America, I learned that food was more than merely fuel for the body; I learned that food can also be medicine for body and soul," Deirdre says.

In fact, Cornucopia began as a health food shop. "We saw that most customers wanted to eat our food on the premises, so that's when we decided to open as a restaurant. For the next fifteen years, the restaurant went from strength to strength – all thanks to the wonder chefs and staff and, of course, Tony Keogh," she adds.

In Cornucopia, the food is all about fresh, seasonal, organic ingredients. "We have always specialised in catering for people with dietary requirements, such as wheat-free, gluten-free and vegan diets, so working with the renal diet was no problem for us and we are delighted to be involved!" Deirdre affirms.

In the kitchen at Cornucopia, chef Tony Keogh is responsible for the wonderful food. "I started my career in restaurants as I worked my way through college, and I loved it, so here I am in still working in the kitchen for the last seven years," he says. Tony has been a vegetarian since he was nineteen years old, before he started working as a chef. "Eating meat just wasn't for me. I lived on cheese sandwiches and cornflakes for the first few years until I learned more about food and how to experiment with ingredients."

Today, Tony's food philosophy is very different from those early days. "A major part of my food philosophy is experimentation and trying new things. I try not to place cultural and geographical boundaries between ingredients. For example, it is perfectly fine to use tofu, polenta and juniper berries in the same dish once you know what you are doing with them. Seasonality and sourcing local food are very important to me, both at home and here in the restaurant.

"At home, I love comfort food. I also like to develop recipes from scratch by combining different flavours and textures. At the moment I am working on some vegan dishes, a terrine set with seaweed, and a schnitzel with an interior made from butter beans and Brazil nuts."

Deirdre adds proudly, "In Cornucopia we have some of the best organic ingredients on the market and I would say that this is the most important element of any recipe. With good ingredients comes great food." Tony couldn't agree more: "Our recipes are all about creating, eating and enjoying good food."

*Cornucopia, 19 Wicklow Street, Dublin 2. Tel: 01 6777583; www.cornucopia.ie*

# Caramelised Onion, Roast Pepper and Brie Tartlet in Thyme Pastry

**Serves 4**

### FOR THE PASTRY

70g (3oz) chilled butter, grated or
    very finely chopped
140g (5oz) plain flour, plus extra for dusting
1 level tbsp fresh thyme, very finely chopped
A pinch (¼ level tsp) of freshly grated nutmeg
25ml (1fl oz) water

### FOR THE CARAMELISED ONIONS

1 tbsp olive oil
2 large red onions, thinly sliced
2 cloves
⅛ level tsp freshly ground black pepper

4 x 10cm (4in) tart tins

### FOR THE RED PEPPER PURÉE

30ml (1fl oz) olive oil
2 red peppers, quartered, deseeded
    and roughly chopped
3 garlic cloves, unpeeled
4 tsp red wine vinegar
80g (3¼oz) Brie made with pasteurised milk

2 bay leaves
½ level tsp brown sugar
1 tsp fresh lemon juice

First make the pastry: rub the butter into the flour until the mixture comes together like fine breadcrumbs. Stir in the thyme and nutmeg, then add the water and bring the pastry together. Wrap it in clingfilm and leave to rest in the refrigerator.

Meanwhile, add a little olive oil to a heavy-based saucepan and place over a high heat. Now add the red onions to the hot oil. Stir vigorously for about two minutes and lower the heat to medium. Add the seasoning; cloves, pepper, bay leaves and brown sugar and then leave to gently sweat for 20 minutes. After this, stir in the lemon juice and set aside. The lemon will bring out the colour of the onions. Once cooked remove and discard the cloves.

On a lightly floured surface thinly roll out the pastry and use to line tartlet tins. Press the pastry into shape. Use the rolling pin to roll over the top of the tartlets and remove any excess bits of pastry. Line the shells with parchment paper and fill them with rice or dry beans to keep the pastry in place while "blind" baking. Set aside to rest in the fridge for 10 minutes.

Preheat the oven to 200°C/400°F/Gas 6. Now make the red pepper purée. Quarter, deseed and roughly chop the peppers. Place them in a roasting tin with the garlic, coat in

a little olive oil and roast them in the oven for about 20 minutes. Remove the garlic after about 15 minutes. Peel it and set it aside. When the peppers are ready, add to a food processor and blend them with the vinegar and garlic. When the mixture is smooth, slowly trickle in the rest of the olive oil, while the processor is on its slowest setting. Once all the oil is combined, stop whizzing and set the purée aside.

Slice the Brie into 4 equal-sized slices.

Now you are ready to "blind" bake your pastry shells. Bake the parchment-lined shells for 7 minutes in the oven. After this remove the parchment and dried beans and place the shells back in the oven for a further 3 minutes.

Remove the pastry shells and using the back of a spoon smooth a quarter of the red pepper mixture into each tartlet case. Follow this with a quarter of the caramelised onions and finish with a slice of Brie. Bake the tartlets for 10–15 minutes until the cheese is beginning to brown nicely.

 ***Per portion*** *this dish provides 2 portions of vegetables and ½ a dairy exchange.*

*Brie is a soft cheese. To ensure food safety it should be made with pasteurised milk and cooked thoroughly; i.e. make sure it is steaming hot all the way through.*

*Check your daily allowances to see if you have enough remainng for this dish.*

# Savoy Cabbage and Barley Broth

**Serves 6**

100g (3½oz) pearl barley
4 bay leaves
1 tbsp olive oil
1 onion, finely chopped
1 carrot, finely chopped
1 leek, finely chopped
1 celery stick, finely chopped
½ level tsp freshly ground black pepper

1 level tbsp fresh thyme, finely chopped
2 garlic cloves, finely chopped
1.5 litres (2½pt) vegetable stock
   (use 1 suitable vegetable stock cube
    to 1.5 litres of water)
200g (7oz) Savoy cabbage leaves, roughly chopped
15g (½oz) fresh flat-leaf parsley

Before using the pearl barley rinse it under cold water. Now add it to a pot containing about 3 times its weight in water. Add 2 of the bay leaves, bring to a simmer and allow to cook for about 1 hour until tender. When it is cooked strain it, then rinse it and set aside.

Meanwhile, coat a heavy-based saucepan with the olive oil and sweat the onion, carrot, leek and celery for about five minutes. Add the garlic, remaining bay leaves, thyme and black pepper and sweat for a further minute. Add the water and stock cube and bring to the boil. Leave to simmer for about 10 minutes until the vegetables are tender.

Meanwhile, blanch the cabbage in boiling water for 3–5 minutes. Stir it, along with the pearl barley, into the broth. Remove a dense ladleful of the mixture, blend it in a bowl with the parsley using a stick blender and then stir all back into the broth. Bring it back to the boil and then remove it from the heat.

Serve the soup immediately in warmed bowls so it retains its bright green colour.

 **Per portion** *this dish provides 2 portions of vegetables.*

*Do not use a homemade vegetable stock. Ask your dietitian to suggest a suitable stock cube. Some of your vegetable allowance has been used to allow the inclusion of vegetable stock in this recipe and therefore we do not recommend that you use it on a regular basis. If you are on a fluid restriction remember to count this soup as part of your daily intake.*

*Check your daily allowances to see if you have enough remaining for this dish.*

# Roast Aubergine and Gran Moravia Mousse with Beetroot Cream, Spiced Couscous, Green Beans, Pan-fried Courgettes and Chickpeas

**Serves 6**

### FOR THE MOUSSE

200g (7oz) aubergine, peeled

4 garlic cloves, unpeeled

3 eggs, separated

A pinch (¼ level tsp) freshly ground black pepper

100g (3½oz) Gran Moravia
    (vegetarian Parmesan made with
    pasteurised milk), freshly grated

100g (3½oz) cream cheese made with
    pasteurised milk

olive oil, for greasing

### FOR THE BEETROOT CREAM

20g (¾oz) butter

100g (3½oz) cooked beetroot (vacuum packed)

1½ tbsp water

120g (4oz) sour cream

10g (⅓oz) fresh dill

1 tsp balsamic vinegar

### FOR THE COUSCOUS

40ml (1½fl oz) olive oil

150g (5oz) couscous

150ml (5fl oz) boiling water

160g (5½oz) courgette, sliced into half-moons

80g (3oz) green beans, trimmed and halved

1½ x 400g (14oz) cans of cooked chickpeas,
    drained and rinsed (approx 345g (12oz))

1 level tsp ground cumin

½ level tsp ground cinnamon

15g (½oz) red chilli, seeded and finely chopped

10g (⅓oz) fresh mint, finely chopped

½ level tsp ground turmeric

2 tsp freshly squeezed lemon juice

6 x ramekin dishes

To make the mousse, preheat the oven to 200°C/400°F/Gas 6. Roast the aubergines with the garlic until soft for about 20 minutes. When they are ready, peel the garlic and place it in a food processor with the aubergines, egg yolks, black pepper, Gran Moravia and

cream cheese and blend to a smooth purée. In a separate bowl, whisk the egg whites into soft peaks and gently fold them bit by bit into the aubergine mixture.

Grease and line the ramekin dishes with parchment paper and carefully divide the mixture between them. Place the ramekins in a deep oven dish and pour hot water into the dish to come halfway up the outside of the ramekins. Bake the mousse in this bain marie in the middle of the oven for about 20 minutes or until each mousse has risen and is slightly springy in the middle to the touch.

While the mousse is baking, you can prepare the couscous. In a bowl add 1 tablespoon of the olive oil to the couscous and ensure each grain gets coated in oil. Then add the boiling water and leave to soak for a few minutes before fluffing the mixture with a fork. Slice the courgettes into half-moons and pan-fry in another tablespoon of the olive oil on a hot non-stick pan, turning once to ensure they are evenly cooked. This should take about 2 or 3 minutes. Blanch the green beans in boiling water for 3 minutes. Refresh under cold water.

Fluff up the couscous once more with a fork, add the chickpeas, cooled green beans and the pan-fried courgettes. Set aside.

To make the beetroot cream, melt the butter in a small saucepan and add the beetroot and water and sweat for about five minutes over a medium heat. Add this into a food processor along with the sour cream, dill and vinegar. Process until smooth.

To finish the couscous, heat the rest of the olive oil and when hot stir in the cumin, cinnamon, turmeric and chilli. Allow to foam a little and stir briefly to stop the spices from sticking. Then add to the couscous mixture with the mint. Stir to combine and allow to warm through.

Remove the aubergine mousses from the oven. Take them out of the bain marie and leave them to cool for about 3 minutes before upturning them into the centre of each plate.

Using a tablespoon drop a quarter of the beetroot cream on to the side of the plate beside the mousse; and using the spoon drag it about 4/5ths the way around the mousse and let it taper off.

Divide the couscous mixture into 6 and spoon it evenly around each mousse following the line, volume and shape of the beetroot cream; serve immediately.

 *__Per portion__ this dish provides 2 portions of vegetables, 1 protein exchange and 1 dairy exchange.*

*Check your daily allowances to see if you have enough remaining for this dish.*

# Fricassée of Summer Vegetables and Baked Tofu in a Sour Cream, Roast Garlic and Butterbean Sauce

**Serves 4**

400g (14oz) tofu
1 bulb garlic, unpeeled
1½ tbsp olive oil

**FOR THE VEGETABLES**
40g (1½oz) butter
1 tbsp sunflower oil
100g (3½oz) red onion, sliced thinly
2 bay leaves
¾ level tsp celery seeds
100g (3½oz) carrot, sliced into batons
100g (3½oz) yellow pepper, seeded and sliced thinly
1 level tbsp fresh thyme, finely chopped
A pinch each (¼ level tsp) of freshly grated nutmeg, turmeric and ground clove
500ml (18fl oz) water
100g (3½oz) green beans
50g (2oz) courgette, sliced at an angle into half-moons
300g (10oz) canned butterbeans, drained and rinsed
10g (⅓oz) fresh tarragon, finely chopped
150ml (5fl oz) sour cream
A pinch (¼ level tsp) freshly ground black pepper

Preheat oven to 200°C/400°F/Gas 6. Rinse and chop the tofu into 1cm (½in) cubes, place them in an ovenproof dish with the olive oil and mix well to coat the tofu. Bake them in the oven along with the head of garlic (leave the garlic head unpeeled, just coated in a little oil). The tofu and garlic should be ready in about 15 minutes. The tofu will need to be turned once during cooking to prevent it sticking as it expands. Once cooked, remove from oven and set aside.

Then, in a large saucepan over a medium heat, melt the butter in the sunflower oil. When it begins to foam add the onions, bay leaves and celery; sweat for a minute or two. Then add the carrot, peppers, thyme and the spices along with the water, stirring to combine. Continue to cook for a further 10 minutes until the vegetables are tender.

Meanwhile, peel the roast head of garlic and add it to a food processor along with the butterbeans. Blanch the green beans in boiling water for 3 minutes and then refresh them under cold water. Add the sliced courgettes to a hot frying pan that has been coated with a drop of oil. Fry for a minute or two, turning once. Set aside.

Strain the cooking liquid from the vegetable mixture and add it to the food processor. Blend it all to a smooth paste and pass it through a sieve back into the vegetable mixture. Be careful to pass as much of the mixture through as possible.

Now add the finely chopped tarragon to the sour cream with the black pepper and stir it into the vegetables. Add the green beans, courgettes and tofu and bring the mixture back to a simmer.

This dish is delicious served with basmati rice.

 *Per portion* this dish provides 2 portions of vegetables and 2 protein exchanges.

*Check your daily allowances to see if you have enough remaining for this dish.*

# Orange Syrup Polenta Slice

**Serves 8**

**FOR THE CAKE**

175g (6oz) butter, at room temperature

125g (4½oz) caster sugar

2 eggs, whisked

200g (7oz) rice flour, available in delis and
     health food shops and better supermarkets

75g (3oz) polenta

1½ level tsp baking powder

100ml (3½fl oz) orange juice

Juice of half a lemon

**FOR THE SYRUP**

100g (3½oz) sugar

50ml (2fl oz) water

100ml (3½fl oz) orange juice

**FOR THE ICING**

150g (5oz) cream cheese made with
     pasteurised milk

125g (4½oz) icing sugar

1 tbsp orange juice

Preheat the oven to 180°C/350°F/Gas 4.

Firstly make the cake. In a large bowl using an electric hand whisk (or you can use a food mixer) cream together the butter and sugar until light and fluffy. Slowly add in the whisked eggs to avoid curdling. Make sure everything is well combined.

Then gently fold in the rice flour, polenta, bread soda and orange juice, again making sure everything is well combined. The mixture may look a little curdled at this stage but don't worry, that's okay.

Using a palette knife, spread the cake mixture evenly onto a parchment-lined oven tray that is approximately 26 x 18cm (10 x 7in) in size. Bake on the middle shelf of the oven for 30 minutes.

Meanwhile, make the icing. In a large bowl or in a food mixer, whisk together the cream cheese, icing sugar and orange juice until well beaten. The mixture should be slightly stiff and smooth looking. Leave, covered with clingfilm, in the refrigerator to chill.

When the cake comes out of the oven leave it to cool for at least 15 minutes before turning it out of the baking tray. The easiest way to do this is to use 2 chopping boards (or large plates). Place one on top of the cake and upturn it. Peel off the parchment paper and then place the other chopping board on the underside of the cake and flip it over.

While the cake is cooling make the syrup. In a small saucepan, bring the syrup ingredients to the boil, lower the heat and cook the mixture until it has reduced by half.

Using a skewer mark the cake at regular intervals. Now pour the syrup slowly and evenly over the surface of the cake. Leave it to absorb for about 20 minutes.

Now using a palette knife spread the icing evenly over the cake. Refrigerate before slicing to serve.

 **Per portion** *this dessert provides ½ a portion of fruit.*

*Baking powder is not suitable if you are on a low-phosphate diet.*

*Check your daily allowances to see if you have enough remaining for this dessert.*

# Plum and Cherry Clafoutis

**Serves 8**

60g (2½oz) butter
3 level tbsp brown sugar
600g (1¼lb) plums, washed,
    halved and stones removed
200ml (7fl oz) milk
200ml (7fl oz) cream

2 tsp vanilla essence
8 eggs
330g (11½oz) caster sugar
2 level tbsp rice flour
300g (10½oz) cherries, washed,
    halved and stones removed

120g (4oz) crème fraîche, to serve
2 level tsp fresh mint, chopped, to decorate

Preheat the oven to 180°C/350°F/Gas 4.

Place the butter and brown sugar together in a large ovenproof dish. Place in the oven for a few minutes to melt the butter.

Toss the plums into the dish with the melted butter and sugar until well coated. Put the dish back in the oven for about 10 minutes, removing to turn once, until the plums are nicely caramelised.

Bring the milk and cream to the boil in a pan with the vanilla essence. Set aside.

Beat the eggs and the sugar together in a large bowl until light and fluffy, then fold in the rice flour. Now add the warmed milk and vanilla mixture very slowly to the egg mixture to avoid it curdling.

Loosely scatter the cherries over the plums and carefully pour over the custard. Bake in the oven for about 30 minutes until risen and lightly browned. Allow to cool a little before serving with a nice dollop of crème fraîche speckled with some finely chopped mint.

***Per portion*** *this dessert provides 2 portions of fruit and 1 protein exchange.*

*While you don't usually think of desserts as having a lot of protein, this recipe has 1 egg per portion and therefore it has been counted in the protein allowances for this recipe. If you have a daily allowance of dairy products, please note that there is milk in this recipe, which needs to be taken from your allowance.*

*Check your daily allowances to see if you have enough for this dessert.*

# The Restaurant Chefs

*The Restaurant Team – Lee Bradshaw, David Workowich, John Healy,*
*Vivian Reynolds, Louise Lennox and Stephen McAllister*

# The Restaurant Chefs.

"The Restaurant" is one of the most popular programmes on RTÉ One television. In each episode a celebrity head chef takes on the culinary challenge to produce a top class, three-course meal with two value-for-money wines. The celebrities who become chefs for a night are people who have a passion for food and dining. The programme gives the "chef" the opportunity to go pro for one night and serve up a real restaurant meal. The resident critics are Tom Doorley and Paolo Tullio, with one other special guest critic each week. The identity of the mystery chef will remain secret to all in "The Restaurant" until after the meal. Before the chef leaves the kitchen the critics will decide whether the meal is worth a star rating of between one and five. When the celebrity chef's identity is revealed they sit down with the critics to find out how they fared.

The professional chefs who mentor the celebrity guest chefs on the show are David Workowich, Stephen McAllister and Louise Lennox. David specialises in starters, while Stephen is in charge of mains and Louise looks after desserts.

And now all three chefs have turned their attention to the renal diet to create the following enticing recipes for *Truly Tasty*.

A Word From…

# TOM DOORLEY

*The Restaurant* critic

This is a remarkable book. Remarkable not just in its concept but in the way that it contains the thoughts and hard work of so many of our best chefs. And also in the way that it underlines how dietary restrictions can amount to an exciting challenge rather than a negative hurdle.

The people whose recipes appear here have one thing in common. They see good food as something to be celebrated, as an integral part of living life to the full. I am hugely impressed, as I am sure you will be too, by the way in which they have responded to the dietary challenges that face people for whom kidney disease is part of daily life.

This is a book that will bring joy into the lives of people who may have felt deprived of some familiar comforts in the kitchen – because it underlines how much pleasure there can be in a diet low in salt, phosphates and potassium.

It's also a beautiful book and not just because of the delicious images it contains. The beauty lies also in the generosity of the people who have put so much time and thought into its production.

*Truly Tasty* is truly a remarkable achievement.

Tom Doorley

Dave Workowich

# Dave Workowich

## *Seasonal and Local*

Some would say that growing up surrounded by good food from around the world is as close to heaven as one can get. When Dave Workowich was growing up in Montreal, Canada, he was exposed to good food every day. "My mother worked for a catering company and, on the days that she had to work away from home, I would be sent to one of the neighbours while she was at work. Now, our neighbours just happened to be Italian, Portuguese and Greek, so you can imagine all the good food and all the great cooking that I got to experience."

It was no surprise really that Dave decided to follow his mother into the world of catering. "I started with the company that my mother worked for and, for eleven years, we catered for G8 summits, F1 Grand Prix and lots of other large events. Then I was offered a job with a chain of restaurants in the Far East so I set off for Hong Kong."

After a few years learning about Eastern cuisine, Dave arrived in Ireland and set up his own restaurant called Fusion in Carlingford. "When I came to Ireland, I met up with some friends who are also chefs and there was this event called 'Big Billy's mushroom hunt' in Avondale, Co. Wicklow. Over lunch, Regina Lubby from RTÉ was recording for her radio show. She asked me if I would be interested in doing a radio show with her, so I did."

From this radio show, Dave was asked to take part in the TV show *The Restaurant*. "I was delighted. I have to admit that I didn't know much about the show, as I don't watch much TV, but it has turned out to be great fun and I have met some fantastic chefs. And working with Louise and Stephen has been great."

On *The Restaurant*, Dave handles the starters, and his love of good food shows in each episode. "For me, food has to be seasonal and local. With all the farmers' markets around the country now, it is much easier to get good locally produced food."

This philosophy of finding local food is very important to Dave. "I love working with local produce; I think we all have to get back to basics. When I started out cooking, I did the fine-dining thing for a while – which has its place – but now more and more people are moving back to well-prepared, simple food, and that's really what it's all about."

When it comes to his favourite basic food styles, for Dave it would have to be Italian and Greek. "I grew up eating good basic Italian and Greek dishes – nothing too complicated, just good ingredients served simply. Great food is an event: food, to me, means bringing people together."

And Dave's recipes for this book are designed to do just that. "I found the list of approved ingredients very interesting and it made me think about how I could look after my own diet. With my recipes, I hope people will just enjoy the whole idea of cooking and sharing their meals with friends and family."

*www.rte.ie/tv/therestaurant*

# Pan-Seared Tuna Fillet with Spicy Tropical Fruit Salsa

**Serves 4**

**FOR THE TUNA**
400g (14oz) fresh tuna, cut into 4 equal portions
4 tbsp extra virgin olive oil
Juice of ½ lime

**FOR THE MANGO VINEGAR**
75g (2½oz) ripe mango, peeled, stoned and diced
30ml (1fl oz) white wine vinegar (6% acidity or lower), plus a little extra if necessary
30ml (1fl oz) water
110g (4oz) sugar
1 Vanilla pod, seeds only (or ¼ tsp vanilla extract)

**FOR THE SPICY TROPICAL FRUIT SALSA**
175g (6oz) fresh pineapple, peeled, core removed cut into 5mm dice
175g (6oz) fresh mango, peeled, stoned and cut into 5mm cubes
175g (6oz) fresh papaya, peeled, seeded and cut into 5mm cubes
15g (½oz) red chilli, seeded and finely minced
1 level tbsp red onion, minced
½ level tsp root ginger, finely grated
Mango vinegar (from above)
1 level tbsp fresh coriander, finely chopped
½ level tbsp fresh mint, finely chopped

To prepare the mango vinegar, bring the water and sugar to the boil and add the vanilla seeds. Continue to boil for just two minutes. Remove from the heat and add the vinegar and finely diced mango. Pour this into a jug blender and puree into a smooth paste.

To cook the tuna fillets, heat a griddle pan until smoking. Brush tuna fillets with olive oil and lime juice, season with freshly ground black pepper. Sear tuna on a hot non-stick griddle pan over medium high heat for 5 minutes on both sides, until cooked through. Remove from heat and set aside.

* Please note the garnish of mint in the photograph was included for illustration purposes only.

To prepare the spicy tropical fruit salsa, combine all salsa ingredients in a bowl and mix well.

To serve, lay out the plates. Place a small mound of salsa in the centre of each plate. Place a tuna fillet on top of each mound and spoon over some more of the salsa, and drizzle a little around each plate. Serve at once.

 **Per portion** *this dish provides 2 portions of fruit and 3 protein exchanges.*

*Check your daily allowances to see if you have enough remaining for this dish.*

# Salad of Roast Beetroot with Garlic Cream Cheese

**Serves 4**

### FOR THE CARAMELISED ONION VINEGAR

1 tbsp extra-virgin olive oil

1 large onion, finely chopped

A pinch (¼ level tsp) freshly ground black pepper

120ml (4fl oz) white wine vinegar

30ml (1fl oz) water

½ level tbsp fresh thyme, finely chopped

### FOR THE ROAST BEETROOT SALAD

200g (7oz) beetroot

3 tbsp extra-virgin olive oil

2 tbsp caramelised onion vinegar (from before)

60g (2oz) mixed baby green salad leaves (may include butterhead, boston, bibb, webb, cos, romaine, iceberg, red leaf and rocket. Avoid spinach leaves.)

120g (4oz) cream cheese made with pasteurised milk

1 clove of garlic, crushed

1 level tsp fresh chives, finely chopped

To prepare the caramelised onion vinegar, heat oil in a large pan until almost smoking. Add onion, reduce the heat to medium or medium-low and sauté for 30 minutes; be careful to stir well and regulate temperature so onions caramelise well and do not burn. Season with fresh ground pepper to taste. Transfer to a blender and purée with the vinegar. Thin with water so the mixture is the texture of a very smooth sauce. Add the thyme and pulse the mixture to blend. Store in an airtight jar. The vinegar will keep for 5 days.

To prepare the salad, preheat the oven to 200°C/400°F/Gas 6. Brush the beets with 1 tbsp olive oil and place in a baking dish. Bake beets for about 1–2 hours, until they are very tender. Once cooked through, remove and leave to rest until cool enough to handle.

Meanwhile to make the garlic cream cheese, place the cheese in a bowl and add the crushed garlic and chopped chives. Mix well and then set aside.

Peel the beetroots and slice very thinly. Arrange slices slightly overlapping in a petal pattern on each salad plate. Drizzle each plate with 1 tablespoon olive oil and half tablespoon caramelised onion vinegar. Toss salad greens in a bowl with 2 tablespoons olive oil and 1 tablespoon caramelised onion vinegar and freshly ground black pepper.

To serve, arrange a small pile of dressed salad leaves in the middle of the beets and add a quenelle (a decorative egg-shape) of garlic cream cheese on top of the bed of leaves.

 ***Per portion*** *this dish provides 2 portions of vegetables.*

*Check your daily allowances to see if you have enough remaining for this dish.*

Stephen McAllister

# Stephen McAllister

## Cooking or Football?

When he was growing up, Stephen McAllister loved Sundays because that's when he got to cook. "My grandfather was a really good cook – I think he had been a cook in the merchant navy. Every Sunday the whole family would travel out to his house for lunch and, while all the other grandchildren were playing in the garden, I was inside watching and helping my grandfather with lunch."

Food always played an important part in Stephen's life as he was growing up. "We didn't grow our own vegetables or keep chickens but we all loved to eat, and sitting down together as a family was, and still is, very important to us all."

So the decision to become a chef was not a difficult one for Stephen. "I decided quite early on that cooking and working with food was what I wanted to do. It was either cooking or football – and it turned out I was better at cooking." In Transition Year, Stephen was sent to QVII restaurant in Dublin and immediately he knew that this was where his future lay. "I just loved the whole experience so, when I left school, I got a job at Chez Hugo in Donnybrook."

That was 15 years ago; today Stephen has his own restaurant, The Pig's Ear, on Nassau Street in Dublin, where he describes his food as simple, good, honest Irish cuisine. "After all these years, I think people like getting back to basics, and that's what I like to do – cook really good, tasty food where the ingredients are top class and as little as possible is done to them. I have worked in a lot of fine-dining restaurants, and that type of cuisine has it place, but it's not for everyone. Here at The Pig's Ear, we are all about good simple food; we cook fine food but it's not fancy food. I like to think we are very approachable – we don't care what people wear just so long as they like good food."

In his home kitchen, Stephen loves to cook Italian. "I love pasta, but you can't beat a good roast chicken dinner with all the trimmings." Of course, Stephen will always be known as the chef who cooks the mains in the popular television series *The Restaurant* on RTÉ. "I love the show but it is hard work. It's all about long days – in fact, it's like starting a new job for every episode, but I absolutely love the whole process."

As for the recipes for this book, Stephen admits he found the process tough, to put it mildly. "The idea was very interesting and it made me think about the different combinations of ingredients. To be honest, I am terrible for not sticking to recipes so I had to be a lot stricter with myself for this project. Above all, I would recommend that people should take pleasure in the whole process. You have to eat – so make sure that the food you choose is good for both your body and soul."

*The Pig's Ear, 4 Nassau Street, Dublin 2. Tel: 01 6703865; www.the pigsear.ie;*
*www.rte.ie/tv/therestaurant*

# Roast Rib of Beef with Roast Vegetables

**Serves 6**

## FOR THE BEEF

1kg (2¼lb) rib of beef joint, for roasting

2 level tsp Chinese 5-spice powder

1 tbsp olive oil

1 small carrot, chopped

1 garlic bulb

2 small celery sticks, chopped

1 small onion, chopped

3 level tsp fresh thyme leaves

1 level tbsp plain flour, for the gravy

300ml (½pt) water

## FOR THE ROAST VEGETABLES

180g (6oz) carrots, peeled and chopped

80g (3oz) parsnips, peeled and chopped

2 small onions, peeled and chopped

4 level tsp softened butter

3 level tsp fresh thyme, chopped finely

A pinch (¼ level tsp) freshly ground
    black pepper

Preheat the oven to 180°C/350°F/Gas 4.

Season the beef on all sides with the 5-spice powder. In a large pan, heat a little oil and add the beef to the hot pan to brown the meat for 1 minute on each side.

Place the vegetables in a roasting tin and lay the beef on top. To cook the beef through to well done, roast it for 1 hour 30 minutes. Baste with the juices every 10 minutes. When the cooking time is up, slice into the middle of the beef to check that the meat is cooked through enough. If not, return it to the oven for a further 10 minutes.

Add the vegetables to the oven to roast for the final 30 minutes of the beef's cooking time. To roast the vegetables, place them in another roasting tin and add the blobs of butter, season with pepper and add the thyme. Roast in the oven until tender; this should take 30 minutes.

Once the beef is cooked, remove it from the tin and place on a plate. Cover with tinfoil and let rest for 15 minutes. Set the roasting dish with its meat juices and gooey vegetables aside to make the gravy.

To make the gravy, place the beef roasting tin with its juices and vegetable remains on top of the hob, over a medium heat. Sprinkle over the plain flour and cook for one minute.

Pour in the water and whisk to blend. Let the water reduce and thicken, stirring or whisking all the time to make sure there are no lumps of flour. Strain the gravy into a clean pot,

discarding all the vegetables. You should be left with rich gravy. Check the consistency; if it's too thick you can add a little more water.

To serve, carve the beef and arrange 125g on warmed plates with the roasted vegetables. Serve the gravy in a warmed jug on the table.

 *The chive mash on p. 44 would go very well with this dish too.*

 **Per portion** *this dish provides 2 vegetable portions, 1½ potatoes (chive mash) and 5½ protein exchanges.*

*If you have a daily allowance of dairy products, please note that there is milk in this recipe (chive mash) which needs to be taken from your allowance.*

*Some of your vegetable allowances have been used to allow the inclusion of vegetable for the gravy in this recipe and therefore we do not recommend that you use it on a regular basis.*

*Check your daily allowances to see if you have enough remaining for this dish.*

# Shepherd's Pie

**Serves 4**

### FOR THE MEAT FILLING

2 tbsp olive oil

450g (1lb) minced lamb

Knob of butter (approx. 20g)

180g (6oz) onions, finely diced

120g (4oz) carrots, finely diced

80g (3oz) celery sticks, finely diced

2 garlic cloves, crushed

25g (1oz) fresh thyme, finely chopped

2 bay leaves

130g (4½oz) tomatoes, chopped

1 tsp Worcestershire sauce

2 level tsp plain flour

600ml (1pt) water

A pinch (¼ level tsp) freshly ground black pepper

### FOR THE MASHED POTATO TOPPING

600g (1¼lb) potatoes (Kerrs Pink or
   Maris Piper are both good for mashing)

125ml (4fl oz) milk

25g (1oz) butter

A pinch (¼ level tsp) freshly ground
   black pepper

A little beaten egg mixture, to coat the top
   of the pie

Place a large frying pan on a medium heat and add a dash of oil to fry off the minced lamb in batches to seal the meat and brown it. Drain the cooked meat through a colander to get rid of any excess fat.

In a separate pan, heat a knob of butter and fry the onions, carrots, celery and garlic. Add the thyme and bay leaves. Cook for 5 minutes. Add the lamb and cook for another 5 minutes. Next add the tomatoes and Worcestershire sauce. Sprinkle with the flour and cook for a a further 10 minutes.

Now add the water and bring to a simmer, then reduce to a low heat and cook for a good hour. Let the stock liquid reduce but don't let it become too thick. If it does, add a little more water. Remove the pan from the heat and discard the bay leaves. Pour the lamb mixture into your pie dish and leave to cool.

While the lamb is simmering you can make the mashed potato. Peel and dice potatoes into 1cm (½in) cubes. Bring to the boil in 10 times their volume of water. Cook until potatoes are soft. While the potatoes are cooking gently warm the milk in a small pan. When potatoes are cooked, drain and return to the warm pan. As you mash the potatoes, add in the warm

milk in stages to make the mash nice and creamy. Finally add in the butter, let it melt and mix in well. Season with black pepper.

Preheat the oven to 180°C/350°F/Gas 4. Spoon or pipe the potatoes on top and brush with a little beaten egg. Bake in the oven for about 30 minutes or until the pie is piping hot and golden brown on top.

 **Per portion** *this dish provides 2 portions of vegetables, 1½ potatoes and 3 protein exchanges.*

*If you have a daily allowance of dairy products, please note there is milk in this recipe, which needs to be taken from your allowance.*

*Check your daily allowances to see if you have enough remaining for this dish.*

# Louise Lennox

## *Baking is a Breeze (If You Have a Good Scales!)*

It was during the eighties that a nine-year-old Louise Lennox got her taste for good food. "My mother, who trained with Le Cordon Bleu, decided to open a small business making pâté and was actually the first person in Ireland to produce Irish pâté commercially. I used to help her – I was nine years of age, and you might call it 'child labour' but that's where my interest in food started!"

At school, given the choice, Louise would read cookbooks whenever she had a reading assignment. "I am quite badly dyslexic and I would read cookbooks all the time so, once a month, my teacher would ask me to bake a cake from my cookery books. That really helped me and, in fact, cooking became my sanctuary. Then the baking bug took hold."

So, from the tender age of nine, Louise knew that all she wanted to be was a chef. "I just knew I wanted to cook. A few weeks before my Leaving Cert, when we were given time off to study, I got my first job as a trainee chef in a little catering firm. From there I got my first real job that paid actual money in Searsons pub in Dublin."

While working in Searsons, Louise enrolled in a three-year cooking course. "I knew I was interested in the pastry side of things, but you need to be fully trained before you can specialise in one area. So, the plan was to work five days a week in Searsons and on my day off to go to college and get my diploma."

After college, Louise spent three years in the pastry kitchen of Maher's Catering followed by a stint working as head pastry chef in Dobbins restaurant in Dublin city centre. Then one day Louise was asked to participate in a radio show. "A journalist for *The Irish Times* wrote an article about me and the next day I was asked to take part in a radio show. From there, the producer of *The Restaurant* contacted me, and the rest is history, really."

As a pastry chef, Louise has a very clear philosophy when it comes to food. "I love food; I have to say, I live to eat. I adore experimenting with food but I also have to have my comfort foods. I love a little bit of everything and I eat dessert every day. My favourite food at the moment is fish, and I have to admit I adore foie gras, but my all-time favourite food is spaghetti bolognese.

"When I saw the list of ingredients for this book, as a chocolate-lover I was a bit disappointed to see it prohibited – but then I saw that eggs, butter and cream were on the list and I knew that, with these ingredients, there would be no problem coming up with really good dishes. For my recipes, all you need is a good weighing scales – once you've got a good scales, baking is a breeze."

*www.rte.ie/tv/therestaurant; louiselennox.ie; Louise's Cakes, Airfield, Dundrum, Dublin.*

# Raspberry and Passion Fruit Mousse

**Serves 6**

4 passion fruits
300g (10oz) fresh or frozen raspberries
2 leaves (3.3g) gelatine
3 egg yolks (pasteurised)*
3 egg whites (pasteurised)*
100g (3½oz) caster sugar
300ml (½pt) fresh cream, softly whipped
30ml (1fl oz) water

Cut passion fruits in half and scoop out the pulp. Put passion fruit pulp and 250g raspberries into a saucepan and cook over a gentle heat until raspberries have softened. Pass through a fine sieve to remove all seeds and allow to cool slightly. Soak gelatine in water for 5 minutes, then squeeze dry and add to raspberry purée, stirring until the gelatine is dissolved.

In a small bowl whisk the yolks and sugar over simmering water until the mixture is thick and pale. Stir in the raspberry and passion fruit purée and gently fold in the softly whipped cream. Whisk the egg whites until they form stiff peaks and then gently fold into the above mixture.

Divide between 6 glasses and allow to set in the fridge, covered with clingfilm, for 2–3 hours. Decorate the glasses with the remaining raspberries to serve.

 **Per portion** this dessert provides 1 fruit portion and ½ a protein exchange.

While you don't usually think of desserts as having a lot of protein, this recipe has ½ an egg per portion and therefore it has been counted in the protein allowances for this recipe.

Check your daily allowances to see if you have enough remaining for this dessert.

* As the eggs are not being cooked thoroughly in the recipe, you should use pasteurised egg to ensure food safety. Pasteurised eggs are eggs that have been heat treated or processed for safety. The eggs should be labelled "Pasteurised". Pasteurised egg is sold in liquid form as whole egg, egg white or egg yolk.

Louise Lennox

# Apple Crumble Ice Cream

**Serves 8**

300ml (½pt) double cream
200ml (7fl oz) milk
6 large egg yolks (pasteurised)
75g (3oz) caster sugar plus 25g (1oz) caster sugar
2 large Golden Delicious apples

50g (2oz) butter plus 40g (1¾oz) butter
1 level tsp ground cinnamon
50g (2oz) plain flour
50g (2oz) light brown sugar
15g (½oz) porridge oats

Place the cream and milk into a saucepan and bring to the boil. In a bowl beat the egg yolks and 75g (3oz) sugar together until pale in colour. Pour the cream and milk mixture on to the egg mixture and whisk. Pour into a clean saucepan and, on a low heat, stir with a wooden spoon until the ice cream custard coats the back of the spoon.

Transfer into a bowl that is sitting in cold water or ice. Leave to cool completely.

Preheat the oven to 180°C/350°F/Gas 4. Put the flour, brown sugar, oats and 40g (1¾oz) butter into a bowl and rub together until it forms a nice breadcrumb texture. Spread out on a baking tray and cook in the oven for 15–20 minutes until golden brown.

Peel, core and roughly chop the apples. Melt the 50g (2oz) butter in a heavy-bottomed frying pan. Then stir in the remaining 25g (1oz) sugar with the cinnamon and apples and cook on a medium heat until apples are soft. Allow to cool. Purée half of the apples and stir into the cooled custard. Churn the mixture in an ice cream maker if you have one. When the mixture is thick, fold in the remaining apples and crumble mix. If you do not have an ice cream machine, place the ice cream mixture in a bowl and freeze until ice crystals begin to form around the side. This usually takes about an hour. Then whisk it again to mix them through and repeat this process five more times.

 ***Per portion*** *this dessert provides ½ a portion of fruit and ½ a dairy exchange.*

*\* As the eggs are not being cooked thoroughly in the recipe, you should use pasteurised egg to ensure food safety. Pasteurised eggs are eggs that have been heat treated or processed for safety. The eggs should be labelled "Pasteurised". Pasteurised egg is sold in liquid form as whole egg, egg white or egg yolk.*

*Check your daily allowances to see if you have enough remaining for this dessert.*

Louise Lennox

# WEIGHT CONVERSIONS

## OVEN TEMPERATURES

| Celsius | Fahrenheit | Gas | Description |
|---------|-----------|-----|-------------|
| 110°C | 225°F | mark ¼ | cool |
| 130°C | 250°F | mark ½ | cool |
| 140°C | 275°F | mark 1 | very low |
| 150°C | 300°F | mark 2 | very low |
| 170°C | 325°F | mark 3 | low |
| 180°C | 350°F | mark 4 | moderate |
| 190°C | 375°F | mark 5 | mod. Hot |
| 200°C | 400°F | mark 6 | hot |
| 220°C | 425°F | mark 7 | hot |
| 230°C | 450°F | mark 8 | very hot |

*For fan-assisted ovens, reduce temperatures by 10°C

## ABBREVIATIONS USED IN THIS BOOK

| 1 tsp | 1 teaspoon |
|-------|-----------|
| 1 tbsp | 1 tablespoon |
| ml | millilitre |
| lt | litre |
| pt | pint |
| g | gram |
| oz | ounce |
| lb | pound |

| VOLUME | | WEIGHT | |
|--------|--|--------|--|
| 5ml | 1 tsp | 10g | ½oz |
| 10ml | 1 dessertspoon | 20g | ¾oz |
| 15ml | 1 tablespoon | 25g | 1oz |
| 30ml | 1fl oz | 50g | 2oz |
| 50ml | 2fl oz | 60g | 2½oz |
| 75ml | 3fl oz | 75g | 3oz |
| 100ml | 3½ fl oz | 100g | 3½oz |
| 125ml | 4fl oz | 110g | 4oz |
| 150ml | 5fl oz (¼ pint) | 150g | 5oz |
| 200ml | 7fl oz (⅓ pint) | 175g | 6oz |
| 250ml (¼ litre) | 9fl oz | 200g | 7oz |
| 300ml | 10fl oz (½ pint) | 225g | 8oz (½lb) |
| 350ml | 12fl oz | 250g (¼kg) | 9oz |
| 400ml | 14fl oz | 275g | 10oz |
| 425ml | 15fl oz | 350g | 12oz (¾lb) |
| 450ml | 16fl oz | 400g | 14oz |
| 500ml (½ litre) | 18fl oz | 450g | 1lb |
| 600ml | 20fl oz (1 pint) | 500g | 18oz |
| 700ml | 1¼ pints | 600g | 1¼lb |
| 850ml | 1½ pints | 700g | 1½lb |
| 1 litre | 1¾ pints | 900g | 2lb |
| 1.2 litres | 2 pints | 1kg | 2¼lb |
| 1.5 litres | 2½ pints | 1.1kg | 2½lb |
| 1.8 litres | 3 pints | 1.3kg | 3lb |
| 2 litres | 3½ pints | 1.5kg | 3lb 5oz |
| | | 1.6kg | 3½lb |
| | | 1.8kg | 4lb |
| | | 2kg | 4½lb |
| | | 2.2kg | 5lb |

**These measurements are approximate conversions only, which we have rounded up or down. It is important not to mix metric and imperial measurements in one recipe.**

# COOKING POTATOES

There are two cooking methods you can use to reduce the **potassium** content in potatoes.

### Method 1: Known as "Double Boiled"

- Peel the potatoes and cut into thin slices.
- Weigh the potatoes and then measure out the water.
  The water used to cook the potatoes must be 4 times the volume of the potatoes. For example: if the potatoes weigh 100g they should be cooked in 400ml of water.
- Add the potatoes and the water to a large pot and bring to the boil.
- Once the water comes up to the boil, strain and discard the water.
- Add the same volume of fresh boiling water to the pot of potatoes and cook until the potatoes are soft through but still holding their shape.
- Once cooked, drain and measure out your allowance before serving.

### Method 2

- Peel and dice the potatoes into 1cm (½in) cubes.
- Bring to the boil in 10 times their volume of water.
- Cook until potatoes are soft, drain and measure out your allowance before serving.

After you cook potatoes, using either method, you can then continue to mash, fry or roast the potatoes as per any given recipe in this book.

Pressure cookers, microwaves and steamers should not be used to cook potatoes, but you can use them to reheat vegetables and potatoes.

**Irish Nutrition and Dietetic Institute**

A Note for Fellow Dietitians

# HOW WE DID IT...

Valerie Twomey came to us with the idea of getting Ireland's top chefs to create bespoke recipes for adults with renal disease and to compile these recipes into a beautifully produced cookbook. She needed our input to ensure that the final recipes were suitable.

We started by providing the chefs with a general list of foods allowed and not allowed, and we included a sample diet sheet.

We divided the group of six enthusiastic renal dietitian volunteers into three groups of two and divided the recipes among the team.

We did a first review where any obvious ingredients which needed to be changed were fed back to the chefs. Then we began the task of analysing each recipe in detail. The aim of the analysis was to provide the user with information to allow them to use the recipes as part of their daily allowances.

We analysed the recipes, focusing on protein, potassium, sodium, phosphate, total fat and saturated fat. This cookery book is best suited for entertaining or for planning that special family meal for adults with chronic kidney disease or those on dialysis. Please note that for most chefs, patients will not have enough in their daily allowances to have a starter, main course and dessert; instead they will have to pick and choose depending on their daily allowances.

**Protein:** Protein exchanges are based on 7g protein exchanges of meat/fish/chicken/egg. A lot of the chefs were quite generous in their portions of meat. For that reason we decided to put in the number of 7g protein exchanges so that the user could choose recipes as part of their daily allowances.

**Potassium:** All fruit, vegetable and potato portions were based on 4 mmoles exchanges of potassium. We probably erred on the side of caution with this nutrient and tended to round up in terms of potassium exchanges e.g. if the potassium content of the fruit or vegetable portion was calculated to be >6.5mmoles it was counted as 2 portions of fruit or vegetable. Also where small amounts of fruit were listed as an ingredient e.g. lemon meringue pie, it was counted as ½ a portion of fruit. We did, on occasion, count the potassium content of fresh herbs and garlic in the vegetable allowances. We also allowed an extra 2 mmoles (approximately) per recipe for "extra ingredients" that is potassium not from daily allowances such as fruit, vegetables, potatoes, meat, dairy or from bread/cereal staples.

**Phosphate:** Dairy exchanges are based on 7g protein exchange e.g. 1 exchange = 200ml glass milk. Where stable foods e.g. scones/brown soda bread were significantly higher than white bread – this was noted and patients were asked to contact their dietitian for further advice.

**Salt:** Each main course dish has less than 1.5g salt which meets current guidelines. www.bda.uk.com/resources/Delivering_Nutritional_Care_through_Food_Beverage_ Services.pdf

**Stock Cubes:** We used Kallo very low salt stock cubes for the purposes of our analysis.

**Fat:** The BDA criteria for a low fat meal (<15g total fat and <5g saturated fat) and for low fat desserts (<5g total fat and <2g saturated fat) was used and where a low fat option was identified they have been marked as such throughout the book. www.bda.uk.com/resources/Delivering_Nutritional_Care_through_Food_Beverage_ Services.pdf

**Weight Conversions:** Weight conversions (from grams to ounces) were undertaken by the editor of the cookbook, Lizzie Gore-Grimes, based on the standard culinary conversion chart (see p. 281). It is important to note that these measurements are approximate conversions only, which have been rounded up or down.

These were altered by us where we felt the conversion was not accurate enough and could significantly affect the potassium content of the recipe.

When portion sizes were not specified by the chef, we analysed using data from the Food Standards Agency, Food Portion Sizes 2nd and 3rd Editions, McCance and Widdowson's *The Composition of Foods*, 6th Summary Edition (2002) and the United States Department of Agriculture (USDA) National Nutrient Database. Some ingredients were also weighed during analysis e.g. chilli.

**Sources of Nutrient Information:** The McCance and Widdowson's *The Composition of Foods* book series, the 6th Summary Edition and supplements was the primary source of data. Where UK data was not available, we used the USDA nutrient database – www.nal.usda.gov/fnic/foodcomp/search/. We would also like to thank the Public Analyst Laboratory in Galway who analysed some foods for us.

Finally we would like to thank Dr Mary Flynn, Chief Specialist Public Health Nutrition, Food Safety Authority of Ireland, for her general advice on food safety queries.

**A Few Words about the Irish Nutrition & Dietetic Institute**

The Irish Nutrition & Dietetic Institute (INDI) is the professional organisation for clinical nutritionists/dietitians in Ireland. Founded in 1968, the Institute has grown steadily and now has over 600 members throughout Ireland and across the world. The INDI's mission is to encourage, foster and maintain the highest possible standards in the science and practice of human nutrition and dietetics, to positively influence the nutrition status and health of the individual and the population in general. This incorporates clinical nutrition, community nutrition, business and industry, research, education and private practice. The INDI was delighted to be involved in this book which will be a fantastic resource for adults with chronic kidney disease.
www.indi.ie

A word from...

## RORY O'CONNELL

# Growing Your Own Herbs

It can't have taken the earliest hunter-gatherers too long to discover the value of wild herbs. The different appearance, aroma and taste of these plants must have fascinated them. We have no way of knowing precisely when humans started to use wild herbs but it's a pretty safe bet to assume that herbs were appreciated for their flavour and curative powers from early on.

Our use of herbs can be traced back to ancient races and right up to the present day. Evidence of using herbs for their medicinal properties has been found in a 60,000-year-old burial site in Iraq, and we know that the ancient Egyptians, Chinese, Greeks and Romans were actively using herbs for medicinal and cooking purposes, as were different cultures from all corners of the globe.

However, what concerns us here is the subject of using herbs in the recipes contained in this book. And the best way to make the most of fresh herbs is to grow your own. Yes, it is a cliché to say, but it really is very easy. Whether you have a garden, patio, hanging basket or windowsill, you can grow your own herbs – and the same goes for vegetables. Apart from the joy of eating the produce, you will also have the added pleasure of enjoying the colour and vibrancy that the plants will bring to your garden. Both herbs and vegetables can be just as pleasing to the eye as more conventional shrubs and plants in the flower garden. All you need is a little enthusiasm.

There has never been more information available to the intimidated amateur on this subject. Every bookshop now has an entire section devoted to gardening and growing edible plants. Most of the weekend newspapers also have a gardening section and the trend in these articles is towards giving more information on vegetable and herb growing. The internet is, of course, also a great source of information.

Go to your local garden centre and chat to the experts there. And remember that, generally, when you plant something, it *wants* to grow and flourish. The more you know about its favoured conditions, the better the plant will grow. Gather together a couple of pots, a windowbox, even an old bucket, some sharp stones, compost and the plants – and you will be in business.

## Here is a simple and practical way to get started

- If planting into containers, make sure there are a few drainage holes in the bottom. These will prevent your plants from getting water-logged.
- It also helps if the containers for planting are not too small or too shallow, as larger, deeper ones hold more compost and take longer to dry out. Add in a few small, sharp stones to aid drainage.
- Fill with organic compost, leaving plenty of room for the herb plant. Make sure the plant is well soaked before planting. If it feels light and looks dry, soak it in its container, in a large basin of water, for an hour until it is thoroughly moist and feels heavy. Be sure to water the compost well before planting.
- Remove the herb carefully from its plastic and pop it into the compost-filled container. It should be planted to the same depth as it was in its original plastic container.
- Cover with more compost, nearly to the top of the container. Firm it in gently by pressing all around the base of the plant with your hands to steady it in place. Water again and don't forget to water regularly.
- Give the plants a few weeks to get established before harvesting and use a scissors when gathering the herbs for cooking.

Rosemary, thyme and sage are hardy and will survive almost any weather conditions. Chives will die back with a bit of severe winter weather. The parsley, which lasts for two years, will continue to grow throughout the winter but will need replacing after its second year of growth. Mint and oregano are semi-hardy and you will have them from spring until the early autumn. The more tender plants, such as basil, need lots of warm sunshine and are really there just for a few months during the summer. A word of warning, though: herb growing can become addictive and even some of our most notable gardeners are replacing some of their specimen plants with herb plots and raised beds for vegetables.

Once you get going with your herbs, the logical step is to move on to growing a few vegetables. You will by now know how a dish can be greatly improved by the addition of fresh herbs and, if you have your own vegetables to boot, your cooking will be transformed. Growing vegetables is, of course, more demanding work than growing herbs, but the rewards are great. You can be creative with container growing if you are short of space – I have grown potatoes successfully in an old bucket!

The other options are allotments or a community garden. There may be a waiting list for an allotment in your area but if you live near a community garden, this can be a great

entry point to growing your own. In community gardens, information and knowledge is shared, as are seeds, plants and, most importantly, the produce. Working as part of a group can be great fun – the heavier, back-breaking tasks can be shared and don't seem nearly as daunting if there are a few pairs of hands involved.

We now know all too well that we must mind this precious planet of ours much better than we have been doing – so if some of your herbs and vegetables can come from your balcony or garden, rather than the other side of the world, you will be doing your bit to help.

Putting your gloved hands into the soil to grow your own will reward you physically and emotionally, and will give you a greater understanding of the fragility of our beautiful planet, truly making sense of the phrase "getting back to nature". An hour or two pottering with pots and plants might not be the answer to all of life's mysteries but it does at least remind us of some of the simple joys that are a part of life.

## Pairing Herbs with Food

**Beef** – Tarragon, thyme and parsley

**Pork** – Sage, thyme and rosemary

**Lamb** – Mint, thyme, rosemary, oregano and coriander

**Chicken** – Tarragon, chives, basil and coriander

**Fish** – Parsley, dill, chives, basil, thyme and parsley

*Rory O'Connell*

## A Note from the Dietitians

Make sure to wash all herbs thoroughly before use.

Fresh herbs are a wonderful way of boosting the natural flavour of food, especially when you are following a low-salt diet. A word of warning though – if you are on a potassium restriction, herbs contain potassium and therefore should only be used sparingly.

# INDEX

Tony Keogh

David Warkovich

Catherine Leyden.

David McCann

David McCann Paul ... Stephen McAllister Liz Moore

Liz Moore Paule Nee Noel McMeel

Rachel Allen Neven Maguire louise lennox

Eugene Mc Sweeney

louise lennox Clodagh McKenna xx

Leylie Hays

Clodagh McKenna xx Paul McNally Roger Falle Roderick McManon.

Roderick McManon. Rory ... Mc Connell

Rory ... Mc Connell Richie Lorraine ...

Tony Keogh

Keogh David Warkovich Catherine Leyden. David McCann

Leyden. David McCann Paul ... Stephen McAllister Liz Mo

McAllister Liz Moore Paule Nee Rachel Al

Rachel Allen Noel McMeel louise de

Eugene Mc Sweeney Neven Maguire

louise lennox Clodagh McKen